The
Southern Way

David Monk-Steel

The Other Side of the Southern 2
Accidents, Incidents and Occasions

Special Issue 13

www.crecy.co.uk

© 2016 David Monk-Steel

ISBN 9781909328587

First published in 2016 by Noodle Books

All editorial submissions to:
The Southern Way (Kevin Robertson)
Conway
Warnford Rd
Corhampton
Hants SO32 3ND
Tel: 01489 877880
editorial@thesouthernway.co.uk

Print managed in the UK by Jellyfish

Noodle Books is an imprint of
Crécy Publishing Limited
1a Ringway Trading Estate
Shadowmoss Road
Manchester M22 5LH

www.crecy.co.uk

Of related interest

The Southern Way Special Issue No.8
The Other Side of the Southern
Accidents, Incidents and Occasions

This companion book concentrates on fallings-off, bent, busted and bruised vehicles, staff errors and mechanical failures on the Southern Railway and its predecessors since the late 19th century.

ISBN 9781906419806 £16.50

Front cover:
Cannon Street collision, 20 March 1961. This is the damaged leading end of Driving Motor Brake Second No S14449S of 4EPB set No S5225, which was the leading unit of the 8.33am Addiscombe to Cannon Street service, showing that the carriage was tilted as it came into contact with the passing 9.14am Cannon Street to Grove Park empty diesel coaching stock. Although not immediately visible here, some of the coaches of unit No 1014 were thrown on to their side by the collision. The driver of the Addiscombe train had failed to stop at a red signal.

Title page:
The east end of a substantive chalk fall affecting the railway at Folkestone in 1915. The route here was seriously affected by similar earth slips in the late 19th and early 20th century.

Rear cover:
Top left: **The motor bogie from 4EPB No 5031, torn off in the derailment, lies across the down Charing Cross line at Borough Market Junction on 12 August 1958. The bridge parapet has been damaged and the remains of one of the wooden shoe beams with the collector shoe still attached is impaled on one end of it. This area has recently been extensively remodelled to remove the two-track bottleneck in connection with the expansion of Thameslink services.**
Top right: **Trailer Corridor Second No S60542 of 6L DEMU No 1014 is partially tilted and shows signs of the side scrape with the Driving Motor Brake Second of 4EPB No S5225. No S60542 was the eighth coach of the twelve-coach diesel empty stock train, and the first vehicle to be struck. Motor Brake Second No S60028, which was the seventh vehicle, remains upright. There is also a clear view of the fairly new Cannon Street 'C' signal cabin, which was erected after the disastrous fire in the original cabin in 1957.**
Bottom left: **The result of the collision at Tunbridge Wells Central station on 22 December 1958.**
Bottom right: **The snowploughs converted from former 'Schools' Class steam locomotive tenders are seen here during conversion at Eastleigh.** *Mark Abbott*

Contents

Introduction

This book will look at some of the mishaps and other difficulties that occurred on the South Eastern Division of the Southern Railway/Southern Region between 1945 and 1975. To start with let us first consider the origins and activities of that Division, which are probably less generally well known than the Central and Western Divisions.

The Southern Region and particularly the South Eastern Division operated an intensive passenger service in Kent and South East London on a severely restricted infrastructure. London had developed a deep dormitory belt in the 1920s and 1930s that stretched for up to 25 miles from the centre. The railway network from which it was formed had grown from two fiercely competitive rivals, the London, Chatham & Dover Railway and the South Eastern Railway, which had sought to lay down tracks to nearly every important township that the other might also wish to serve. Following the retirement of the two competing Chairmen of these companies, a working agreement was brokered in 1899. The resultant tangle of lines did offer a certain degree of flexibility, but a number of 'pinch points' caused by hurried expansion in earlier years left a legacy of operational difficulties, not least that of Borough Market Junction, just west of London Bridge. These pinch points were to become an operational headache, particularly when accidents occurred, which, given the intensity of the train service, were inevitable.

The South Eastern & Chatham Management Committee, which took over the affairs of the two main rivals, did effect some improvements. It added a few extra link lines, notably at Chislehurst, to permit easier interworking. It also set about introducing new and better rolling stock, and even contemplating electrification. However, all was not to be plain sailing. The Great War (1914 to 1918) put paid to any meaningful developments, particularly because the South East of England, being close to the scene of battle, meant that the railways were heavily over-stretched. The railways were required to move vast quantities of men and material to France and Belgium. There was thus little time or opportunity to upgrade the civilian railway infrastructure.

Above: **This is a fairly typical steam-hauled train in the South East, at Folkestone Warren pre-1940. It is an up Dover express composed of six coaches behind an 'L1' 4-4-0. This stretch of seaside railway, although picturesque, is prone to coastal erosion, and severe falls of the chalk cliffs have obstructed the line on many occasions.**

A common pre-conception is that there is little heavy industry in the South East. Broadly speaking, away from the Thames Estuary this is indeed true, but the South East is an area of significant consumption and trains of coal and other commodities were brought from the north and west to goods yards throughout the region. Here a typical pre-war goods train hauled by one of Harry S. Wainwright's 0-6-0 Class 'C' goods locomotives passes towards Sydenham Hill.

After the Great War the railways were grouped at the insistence of the Government. On 1 January 1923 the South Eastern & Chatham Railway Managing Committee and its constituents were absorbed into the geographically smallest but certainly what was to become the most 'go-ahead' of the 'Big Four' companies, the Southern Railway (SR). The Great War had certainly left its toll on the SR's inherited infrastructure and rolling stock, and it soon set about to put this to rights. It also started to modernise as far as it was able.

From 1926 the Southern Railway had begun to electrify its South Eastern suburban network, using a third-rail DC system originally chosen by the London & South Western Railway in 1915, but in its own inimitable 'make do and mend' style. Only a few of the electric trains supplied to the Eastern Section were really new. Old wooden carriage bodies from four- and six-wheel South Eastern Railway stock were placed end-to-end on new steel underframes, which, as will be seen later, was a factor in accidents. Signalling and track layouts generally were left as they were and although some power-operated colour light signalling was introduced on the immediate approaches to London, much of the network retained semaphore signals and traditional telegraph block signalling. A lot of this signalling dated from the 19th century.

Much had indeed been achieved by 1939 when Britain was at war again across the short sea channel. This was a new kind of war, which brought death and destruction much closer to home. Developments in air warfare were particularly influential, resulting in bombs falling regularly on the railways and adding to the burden they were required to carry. Kent, which again was only a few miles from the 'front line', took the brunt of these attacks and after the 'Fall of France' in 1940 was within actual shell shot of the enemy. Railway lines were blown up, stations, bridges and viaducts demolished and personnel killed, injured or made homeless. Still the Southern carried on making do and mending as it could (as has been told in great detail in other books in the 'Southern Way' series), but its legacy was a tired and run-down railway system. By the time the war had ended in 1945 the network was in a worse state than it had been in 1919.

Work started in 1945 to improve and restore the network, and following nationalisation the newly formed British Railways continued to enhance the railway. BR Southern Region completely replaced the power supply system to the suburban area from 1953, this work almost the equivalent of a re-electrification. A 'Modernisation Plan' was announced in 1955 for the whole of British Railways; this included the route from

Erith station and goods yard, seen here in 1949, served an historic Thames-side town that had established itself as a heavy manufacturing centre in late-Victorian times and therefore required a large goods yard to handle a variety of traffic. Private sidings were connected at a number of locations, principally Crabtree Crossing north-west of the station, Erith goods yard itself, and North End sidings to the south-east. Coal brought by coaster was landed at Erith and moved by train to Lower Sydenham gas works and to other large consumers of fuel.

Charing Cross to Hastings being dieselised from 1957, while Victoria to Ramsgate and Dover via Chatham was electrified in 1959 and via Tonbridge in 1961. Diesel locomotives started to replace steam from 1960, and by 1963 the South East of England was entirely operated by modern traction.

Returning briefly to the origins of the system, the speed of expansion and initial lack of finance at the time that the lines were being laid down resulted in an infrastructure that was not of the finest quality. This was not helped by the geography and geology of the countryside through which it passed. The chalk bed was sound, but above it was clay, sand and gravel, resulting in a legacy of embankment slippages and other major earth movement that wrought havoc, usually at inconvenient moments. The railways had not helped themselves in this respect, and a terrible derailment on 24 August 1927 just north of Sevenoaks was attributed in large part to poor ballast and drainage.

Much of the low-lying land adjacent to the River Thames and the sea coast was prone to mist and fog, which added yet another dimension to the difficulty in operation. The Southern Region had developed sophisticated 'Fog Working' programmes to thin out the train services when things got bad; this helped a

bit, but never enough. Sighting semaphore signals from the footplate of a steam locomotive was a very difficult task. Even though the motorman's cab of an electric train, with improved forward vision, did make this task easier, the thickness of a 'London pea-souper' was never an easy thing to penetrate.

In the following pages I will use examples of accidents to describe what happened when things did go wrong. I will attempt to show what the underlying causes were and to identify trends. Much of the information has been taken from the railway authority's internal investigations known as 'Joint Inquiries' and also the reports of the Railway Inspecting Officers of the Ministry of Transport, who were required by Government to investigate serious accidents on the railway, and to make recommendation for improvement. The period covered is from 1945 until 1975 and the area is that of the South Eastern Division of the Southern Region of British Railways. Before 1 January 1948 the lines were owned and managed by the Southern Railway, a private company, albeit heavily regulated. (Where an official Ministry of Transport enquiry into an accident took place, many of these will be found on the excellent www.railwaysarchive.co.uk site.)

Chislehurst goods yard on the up side north of Chislehurst station is a typical goods yard, with a goods warehouse offering covered accommodation to transfer goods between road and rail vehicles, which can be seen in the middle distance. Ricketts coal merchant is still trading from here in this early 1960s view. Wagons of coal and smokeless fuel arrived daily by goods train. A couple of road vans that would be used to deliver sundries are visible in the yard near the warehouse. These would be taken round the district attached to a Scammell three-wheel 'mechanical horse'. Goods would arrive in either covered vans or open wagons covered with a tarpaulin sheet. Nearest to the camera are six drop-sided ballast wagons loaded with stone ballast. These no doubt are for a local overnight re-ballasting job, in those days still carried out with pick and shovel. All this would be swept away in the following ten years. A 'Coal Concentration Depot' run by Charringtons would shortly be opening in the goods yard at Beckenham Junction only a few miles distant. Sundries traffic would for a time be concentrated at Bricklayers Arms, from where lorries would travel out to local firms. Later still all this traffic would be lost to road. For a period in the 1970s and 1980s Chislehurst became a reception depot for shingle ballast from Lydd, where it would be carried in open high wagons. In more recent years the rails were removed and site covered in tarmac to become a commuter car park.

The Railway Routes and Train Services in the South East – Setting the Scene

The South East of England was served from six main stations in London: Victoria, Holborn Viaduct and Blackfriars were built by the London, Chatham & Dover Railway (LCDR), and Charing Cross, Cannon Street and London Bridge by the South Eastern Railway (SER). London Bridge was shared with the London, Brighton & South Coast Railway; it was a terminus, but was generally a through station so far as the South East was concerned. From here the lines stretched out into Kent, with a prime objective of claiming the cross-Channel business at Dover. From Victoria the LCDR route travelled along the North Downs, then through North Kent to Faversham, via the Medway towns of Rochester and Chatham, whereas the SER passed via Tonbridge and the Kentish Weald. Branches were thrown off from both routes at every opportunity to serve major towns. Therefore both companies had stations in

Greenwich, Gravesend, Rochester, Chatham, Sevenoaks, Maidstone, Canterbury, Margate, Ramsgate and, of course, Dover. Even Whitstable had both the rivals in town, the SER gaining access via the early Canterbury & Whitstable Railway.

This is New Cross station, seen in 1949. It is located on the South Eastern main line between Charing Cross and Lewisham and is the first station after London Bridge. New Cross is on the outskirts of Central London and was a hub for local travellers to the City of London. The Metropolitan Line's East London branch had a terminus here, where travellers could change onto the Underground for Whitechapel and East London. A network of suburban services called here, but main-line expresses ran through non-stop. The headcode 'S' with a white bar over the letter on the front of this electric train – composed of former LBSCR coach bodies mounted on new underframes – indicates that it is a Dartford to Charing Cross service via the Bexleyheath line. It is arriving at Platform 3. Suburban destinations that could be reached from here included Dartford via Blackheath and Woolwich, also via Bexleyheath or Sidcup. Trains from here also went to Bromley North and Sevenoaks via Orpington.

When the working union was agreed in 1898 little actually changed. Some link lines were built where the main lines crossed each other near Chislehurst, but it was not until the conditions of war forced rationalisation in 1915 that any lines were actually shut. Even then it was very lightly used branches that disappeared. The LCDR Greenwich Park* and the SER Chatham Central branches succumbed. The venerable Canterbury & Whitstable hung on somewhat longer, but this too was a casualty first for passengers in 1934, and finally to all services in 1950. Even so, there was generally a good mixture of train services.

Suburban services

Intensive suburban services from Hayes, Addiscombe, Orpington, Bromley and Dartford were electrified from 1926 onwards. The traction supply chosen was the third-rail current collection DC system. This was cheap to lay, but notoriously susceptible to freezing conditions. It was also affected badly by flooding. Trains were formed from multiple units initially of three coaches with a driving position at the outer ends. Apart from a small batch of twenty-five units, all the 'new' trains were created from existing steam-hauled stock, by the simple expedient of removing the old four- and six-wheel underframes and mounting the bodies on new 62-foot-long steel chassis. The motorman's cab was new, and a certain amount of 'cut and shut' of odd compartments or filler pieces had to take place to cater for different lengths of donor carriages. To cater for peak loading in the morning and evening, two units would run coupled together, frequently with the addition of a two-car trailer set sandwiched between. These trailer sets were created by taking steam-stock bogie coaches and fitting them with air brakes, electric lights and through control cables. This in itself created operating difficulties. To save money outside the peak periods, the trains would be reduced to three cars. The remaining five cars, including the trailer set with a blind end outermost, would be left at the buffer stops of terminal bays at Addiscombe, Hayes or Orpington or in sidings at Dartford, Sevenoaks or Slades Green. Shunting trains with a 'blind end' was always less

desirable, and risky. By the time the Second World War was in full swing this inconvenient and potentially dangerous practice was finally discontinued. Good-condition trailer cars from the trailer sets that had standard 62-foot underframes were inserted into the three-car units, bringing them up to four cars, and a batch of new trailer cars to an improved design was constructed to be inserted into the rest. Non-standard carriages and those damaged or worn out were scrapped.

The first batch of new units introduced in 1941 was to Bulleid's design, with a wider body that allowed six persons to sit side-by-side rather than five as in the old all-wooden stock. The body was also clad in steel sheet, but was still on a timber frame with a timber canvas-covered roof. However, a greater safety improvement was achieved in the next and subsequent batches by using a similar body shape but now with welded steel construction throughout. After the war the old wooden-bodied trains were progressively withdrawn, and the underframes, some barely 20 years old, were re-used but now with bodywork to the new 'six-a-side' welded all-steel format. The new units that appeared from 1946 onwards incorporated at least two, and often three, vehicles with an open saloon seat arrangement, which allowed passengers to move between seating bays to find accommodation, and provided extra space to stand if all the seats were taken. On most suburban routes off-peak frequency was intervals of 15 or 20 minutes.

Electrically operated outer-suburban services were added to the South Eastern section in 1939. Semi-fast trains now operated to Gillingham and Maidstone via Swanley or Strood. These replaced steam-hauled services and helped to free up some of the operational problems caused by shunting and running round locomotives at the London termini. The new services were operated with two-coach multiple units (designated 2HAL), which could operate in formations of anything up to ten cars. The design incorporated traditional bodywork construction of steel sheet over a timber frame, and could if necessary operate in multiple with suburban units. The Motor Coach was similar to the suburban stock, albeit with a wider body, but the Driving Trailer incorporated a side corridor giving access to a lavatory for passenger use. A half-hourly off-peak frequency was the norm, with a semi-fast and a stopping service alternating on each route.

Crowds of passengers waiting to board a train five or more deep on the platform are usually associated with the London termini or London Bridge. However, the holiday resorts of Margate and Ramsgate in the days of steam once attracted the crowds, and before the time when most families jetted off to sunnier climes the trains taking them out and bringing them home after their holiday could be full and standing. In the 1970s cheap fares to the seaside revived this interest in train travel, and large numbers of day-trippers travelled mid-week from suburban stations, taking advantage of extra trains being operated using rolling stock that was returning to coastal depots after up morning business services. Unfortunately the stock was needed back in London for the return business peak long before the day-trippers wished to return, so the ordinary services bore the brunt of the extra loads. Scenes like this, where a twenty-four coach load of mothers and children were trying to board a four- or eight-coach train at Margate became common during the years 1974 to 1977. *David Monk-Steel*

* See the article on the Greenwich Park branch in 'SW36'.

On suburban services the South Eastern Division was virtually free of timber-framed carriages from 1958 when the 2HAL Maidstone and Gillingham units were transferred to the Central and Western Divisions to be replaced by similar but more up-to-date outer-suburban electric stock (2HAP) of BR Mark 1 design. The corridor was only provided along the 1st Class section in the driving trailer, and the 2nd Class portion of the unit was an open saloon arrangement. All inner-suburban stock had been rebuilt, or eventually replaced at about the same time by units of similar build (2EPB and 4EPB) especially when ten car working was introduced from 1954 onwards. The electro-pneumatic brake (EPB) was incorporated in all electric stock built after 1951. This had an electrically activated valve in the brake supply system serving the air brakes, which meant that brake application and release was almost instantaneous.

One peculiar suburban electric train deserves a special mention. In 1949 eight coaches designed by Bulleid were introduced between Charing Cross and Gravesend, formed into two four-coach units. They were constructed to the maximum permitted gauge, so that extra seats could be squeezed in between the compartments at a higher level. It was described as a 'double-decker', but was not truly thus as the feet of the 'upstairs' passengers were at about the same level as the heads of those 'downstairs'. A short staircase connected the individual upper and lower compartments, but passengers were required to use a single side door in the lower one. Hailed initially as a means of increasing capacity on the intensively used suburban routes, this train quickly proved to be claustrophobic and very unpopular. To get the maximum width there was no footboard under the door and no commode handle to assist in boarding or alighting. Following a number of accidents to passengers boarding and alighting, and also some assaults on passengers in the upper compartment, the decision was taken not to perpetuate the design. Even so, the two units remained in service until 1972. British Railways decided instead to increase capacity by lengthening platforms and adding two carriages to peak-period suburban trains. More details about the EPB stock and the 'double-decker' were previously published in 'Southern Way' issues 20, 24, 25 and 26.

Express trains

At the start of the period under consideration the longer-distance trains to Ramsgate, Margate, Folkestone, Dover and Hastings remained steam-hauled much as they had been before the war. Trains of ten or twelve coaches were typically made up from a mixture of Maunsell corridor carriages with timber-framed bodywork, together with odd additional carriages ('Swingers'), frequently former SECR ten-compartment 100-seat non-corridors, and occasional vehicles from other sections.

The Eastern Section of the Southern Railway and the South Eastern Division of BR were users of Pullman cars, mainly in the Continental boat expresses, where one or two would be marshalled into the train and available for a supplementary fare. A full train of Pullman cars operated in the summer from Victoria to Margate and Ramsgate, running as the 'Thanet Belle', although for a short period a Dover portion was also conveyed and the title altered to 'The Kentish Belle' to suit. The other all-Pullman train was the 'Golden Arrow', connecting at Folkestone and Dover with ferries to France. For most of its period of operation only Pullman passengers were carried, but in later years some ordinary carriages were substituted for part of the formation.

After the Second World War new rolling stock appeared. Initially this included Bulleid's corridor vehicles that still used timber as a substantial part of the bodywork, particularly the roof, but eventually from 1951 onwards BR Mark 1 corridor stock appeared, which had all-steel bodywork. In the period under discussion the South Eastern Division continued to employ a mixture of all these types, and timber-framed stock was not finally eliminated until 1961, when all the main lines in Kent were finally electrified or for a short period only turned over to diesel haulage with Mark 1 carriages.

Most main lines offered an hourly service of fast trains, with steam-hauled stopping services, serving intermediate stations, following or sometimes detached from the expresses at major junctions. In between these were the 'boat trains' running non-stop from Victoria to Dover or Folkestone. The tidal nature of cross-Channel services meant that numerous train paths were incorporated into the timetable (known as 'Q' paths because of the footnote reference letter use), but diverse routing had to be employed to find a way through, especially in the London suburban area. Boat trains could therefore run via both the LCDR route through Canterbury and Chatham, the SER route via Tonbridge and Sevenoaks, or occasionally via Ashford, Maidstone and Swanley. Charing Cross was rarely used for Continental expresses – the route via London Bridge just couldn't cope. Boat trains nearly always included a four-wheeled van or two for the copious amounts of luggage typical of the period.

One peculiarity was the route between Tonbridge and Hastings. Because of dishonest practice by a contractor when building the line, the tunnels were inadequately lined with brick, and as a consequence started to show signs of collapse. The quick fix for this was to add another lining of brick to reinforce them, but this then left a legacy of tunnels narrower than standard. This was not so much of an issue while carriages were of modest dimensions, but after the Grouping of 1923, as the width of carriages increased, these narrow tunnels became an operating headache. The Southern Railway had to build carriages of limited width for these services, and when in the 1950s these themselves required replacement the new diesel trains were also built to a limited dimension. It is less well known that the North Kent line was similarly restricted, although not nearly so severely, and when the route was required to pass standard-width stock, certain clearance works had to be carried out to allow Southern Railway standard types of locomotive and carriage to pass. Indeed, the South Eastern Division was never able to accept certain ex-LBSCR or LSWR types right up until the end of steam.

Bromley South, seen here in April 1958, was an interchange point between Kent Coast trains from Victoria and local suburban services. At the time the picture was taken the photographer was standing on the down platform so that the lines reading from the far left were the up slow and up fast, with the down fast line just adjacent and the down slow line out of sight to the right of the picture. As a consequence of the Kent Coast electrification planned for June 1959 the lines were resignalled in May 1959 and the directions altered so that the platform to the left was then flanked by the up and down fast lines, and the lines on either side of the platform from which the picture was taken became the up and down slow. This all coincided with remodelling at Shortlands and Bickley and four-tracking from Bickley Junction to Swanley, together with new colour light signalling controlled from new power signal boxes at Shortlands and Chislehurst Junction. Because passengers changed trains here, there are facilities such as a tobacco kiosk and newsagent on the platform.

As well as intensive business traffic into and out of London, the railways of the South East served a gateway to Europe. This therefore provided the opportunity to witness the prestigious trains serving the cross-Channel ferries. Electric locomotive No E5006 is seen here in the early morning on the Catford Loop with the up 'Night Ferry' in the early 1960s. This unique train conveyed through sleeping cars that had come from Brussels and Paris via the Dunkirk to Dover train ferry, as well as ordinary carriages for 'walking' passengers. In the days before jet travel by air became commonplace, this together with the 'Golden Arrow' service were *the* way to visit Europe.

In stark contrast to the hustle and bustle of the London suburbs and major termini there were plenty of sleepy branch lines in the rural South East. Here at Minster in Sheppey on the branch from Queenborough to Leysdown, the quiet ambience is obvious. The station building is a typical Colonel Stephens design, in corrugated-iron sheet. Stephens was the engineer for the construction of the Isle of Sheppey Light Railway. The small goods yard features a loading gauge and contains a single coal wagon. Only the rail-built SR-style signal looks half modern! Trains usually consisted of an ex LCDR 0-4-4T and a pair of push-and-pull carriages, frequently the former 1906 SECR railmotor coach portions articulated as a pair on three bogies. Mixed train working, that is passenger and goods vehicles in the same train, was not uncommon. The branch line to Leysdown was barely remunerative and was prone to road competition. It closed in 1954.

Branch lines

On branch lines, particularly to Allhallows-on-Sea, Westerham, Hawkhurst and Bexhill West, services were in the hands of pull-and-push steam-operated trains. These were formed of two carriages from the pre-Grouping companies with a driving compartment inserted at the end of the brake vehicle and through controls to the tank engine. The fireman remained on the footplate at all times, but the driver could ride either on the locomotive or in the driving trailer car, and operate the brake and regulator from either. These trains also operated a few local services on the main lines and secondary routes such as Paddock Wood to Maidstone West.

Freight services

Freight services were surprisingly heavy and frequent. The Southern was not noted as an area of industrial production, but was certainly one of consumption. Large quantities of traffic passing via the train ferry between Dover and the port of Dunkerque was run at speed to and from the freight termini at Ewer Street or Blackfriars. In 1960 a new Continental Depot was opened at Hither Green on the up side, and these two inner-London depots were abandoned. A privately run fruit distribution depot was eventually built at Paddock Wood.

Considerable goods traffic arrived via the City Widened Lines from the north, and then had to find its way to the marshalling yards at Hither Green or Herne Hill. The North Kent and Medway Valley lines were particularly busy with cement and paper traffic. Erith generated a lot of traffic too, with frequent coal trains from North End sidings to Lower Sydenham gas works. Coal arrived at Erith by sea, and was transhipped to rail using a wharf operated by Cory Brothers. Erith also included much heavy industry and until the 1960s, when road competition finally succeeded in winning this traffic, the goods yard there was always busy.

The Woolwich Arsenal was a major source of railway freight. Plumstead yard was busy with traffic to and from the Arsenal. There was a connection to the Dockyard at Chatham out of Gillingham goods yard, which handled a lot of stores and material for the Navy. In later years this was used for transferring irradiated fuel to and from nuclear submarines, conveyed in an exceptionally large wagon. Nuclear fuel also kept the branch from Lydd to Dungeness alive when a nuclear power station was opened there in the 1960s.

Angerstein's Wharf near Charlton was another entry point, and considerable traffic in timber arrived here. The wharf also housed the Civil Engineer's depot, where track material was received and processed. At Hither Green and at Ashford the Civil Engineer manufactured pre-assembled track panels to keep the rails in good order, and relaying trains departed virtually every weekend with new material, arriving back afterwards with old material for disposal.

There were busy marshalling yards at Dover, Tonbridge, Ashford and Hoo Junction with trunk haulage between them and a radiating web of local services, mostly at night, serving local stations and coal sidings. Most stations had a coal yard where domestic coal was distributed by local coal merchants. A lot of this traffic from the north of London arrived on to the Division over the West London Extension line to Longhedge, then on the South London Line via Nunhead to Hither Green and Blackheath. Following smokeless zone legislation in the mid-1950s, domestic coal traffic changed and finally by 1970 had gone. For a period of time coal depots were concentrated into a number of high-capacity mechanised yards, examples being at Beckenham Junction, Plumstead, Rochester, Southfleet (for APCM) and Maidstone. This allowed higher-capacity hopper wagons to replace more traditional box-bodied vehicles; however, this did not stem the loss, and by 1985 most of this traffic was gone.

In steam days a peculiar traffic consisting of landfill passed from Walworth sidings near Camberwell to a tip near Longfield and Meopham. This was chiefly refuse collected by London County Council and was often highly flammable. Trains of open wagons, usually of wooden construction, were hauled by steam locomotives and, despite the loads being covered with tarpaulin sheets, occasionally the sparks from the engine chimney would set a wagon load ablaze. One trick to counter this was to stop at a station with a water column and douse the smouldering before it got a hold. It was not always successful!

East Kent was at that time also producing coal from four main collieries – Betteshanger, Tilmanstone, Snowdown and Chislet – which was to find its way to all points on the railway network, including flows to coke-producing areas in northern England to 'sweeten' the mixture. Until 1961 nearly all these services were in the hands of steam locomotives.

Other notable freight flows included oil from the Isle of Grain, shingle from Dungeness and Lydd, and gypsum from Mountfield, much of which was taken to Crabtree sidings at Erith or to the North Kent cement works. The branch line from Hoo Junction to Allhallows-on-Sea and Grain closed to passenger traffic in 1961, but remained very busy with freight, as it does to this day. A huge new refinery was opened in 1954 to supplement what was already a small oil storage facility there already. A chemical and oil company, Berry Wiggins, occupied the site of a former airship station at Kingsnorth and had a connection to the branch at Sharnal Street, as too did the Navy stores at Upnor.

Livestock movements included sheep from Romney Marsh, where there was once considerable movement for summer and winter grazing, and horse traffic to the various racecourses, notably Westenhanger near Folkestone. Much of this succumbed to road completion quite early.

Some other remarkable traffic dating from the 1960s and 1970s included imported cars from Ramsgate and Ridham Dock, gravel from Cliffe to Angerstein's Wharf and King's Cross, scrap metal to and from Queenborough and Sheerness, china clay from Burngullow to Sittingbourne and, of course, cement in great bulk from a new cement works at Northfleet opened in 1970. The Northfleet works also received coal in long trains of forty-three of the new 'merry-go-round' wagons hauled by two locomotives from the Midland Region, and gypsum in similar wagons from the mine at Mountfield.

Freight rolling stock

Freight rolling stock remained fairly traditional until the 1970s. From 1948 the steel-bodied 16-ton mineral wagon progressively replaced the timber-bodied (and frequently also timber-framed) former private owner coal wagon for coal traffic. General merchandise travelled in steel-framed vans and open wagons with timber bodies, and in the case of the latter more often than not protected with a tarpaulin sheet. New refineries on the Isle of Grain introduced flows of tank wagons carrying various oil and chemical products during this period. The train ferries conveyed European types of wagon, chiefly long-wheelbase vans, capable of operating at the higher speed necessary for travelling on the 'Grande Vitesse' services.

Ashford Works became a major manufacturer of freight vehicles, especially in the 1960s, and also won export orders for overseas railways. These new vehicles on completion, despite being to a non-standard gauge, passed to the port of embarkation on special accommodation bogies under 'exceptional load' conditions.

This is an Italian ferry van with a distinctive peaked roof, and was used for bringing chilled fruit, vegetables and other produce to Britain via the cross-Channel train ferry. Trains of similar vans were run at fast schedules from the ferry port to London goods terminals at Blackfriars and Ewer Street (near Metropolitan Junction). Rolling stock on mainland Europe was fitted with air brakes, although Portugal and Spain used the vacuum brake like British Railways, and many vehicles had through vacuum pipes, as does this one. This picture was taken in 1940, at which time all ferry traffic had ceased with the fall of France to the Nazis. The vehicle, being trapped in Britain, has been requisitioned by the LNER for internal traffic. In the 1950s many such vans could be observed empty awaiting a return service from St Johns in a siding alongside the up fast line; the site of this siding has since been obliterated by the Lewisham Vale Flyover line. Vans such as these could still be seen in trains on the South Eastern Division into the 1970s.

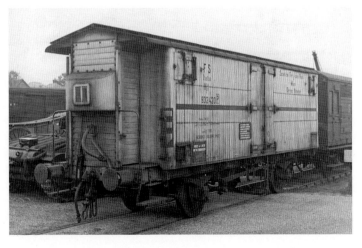

A remarkably rare and unusual train is seen here. No E5007 hauls the prototype RoadRailer train up through Margate. This train was experimental and toured Britain for exhibition purposes. It was based upon an idea originating with the Chesapeake & Ohio Railroad in the USA. The 'wagons' could be moved on road individually as articulated trailers behind a lorry tractor unit, or on rails in a train, nose to tail, with an adaptor wagon between the leading vehicle and the locomotive. There were interchangeable road and rail wheels at the rear of each wagon, while its front end was supported by a coupling either to the wagon in front or to the adaptor wagon. Unfortunately problems were encountered with the RoadRailer couplings, which were never satisfactorily resolved before the Freightliner train concept, which was also on the drawing-board, was adopted as the preferred inter-modal system. The RoadRailer idea was abandoned before entering revenue-earning service.

Parcels and mails

Parcels services were regular on most of the main routes. A network of 'newspaper trains' radiated from London daily from about 3am traversing the main lines and dropping off one or two vans at key junctions. Newspaper sorters travelled in these vans, to unload the various editions to the waiting newsagents at the stations en route. The General Post Office was heavily committed to the railway for letter and mail services, but especially approaching Christmas, when there was a huge volume of traffic both in ordinary passenger services and in special mail trains. BR too still had a thriving parcels business, including collection and delivery services at principal stations. Much of this still travelled in Southern Railway-designed vans made of timber on a steel framework. Electric trains had large luggage compartments normally rated to convey a ton of mail or parcels traffic, with the additional note 'evenly distributed'. The consequence of all of this was that at many stations, especially the London termini, there were mountains of boxes and bags for both passengers and staff to negotiate!

Most principal stations had a 'road motor' or two (this old term for a motor lorry was in use for decades) for parcels and sundries deliveries. Bricklayers Arms was the chief depot for the South Eastern in the London Area, and was a major marshalling and re-sorting point. London Bridge Low Level was also a mail and parcels handling point, especially in the run-up to Christmas. As time went on parcels concentration into larger and fewer depots took place, but Canterbury East, for example, was still handling large quantities of railway parcels traffic into the mid-1970s.

The South Eastern Division was not a huge carrier of milk, although milk trains did run in from other areas. A bulk depot was erected in the goods yard at Mottingham for the reception of milk in bulk tank wagons, but otherwise most of this traffic came in vans and was conveyed in churns. For a time a service from Yeovil to Gravesend arrived via Tonbridge and the Medway Valley with milk cans, which were then transferred to ordinary train services.

Fruit, vegetables and hops

Fruit and vegetables were a particular seasonal traffic with special trains run during the late summer and autumn, especially for cherries, apples and pears. These trains would stop at stations in between the normal passenger services and there would be a huge effort by the staff to load the fruit and avoid delay. Speed was always of the essence. Stations like Teynham, for example, suddenly became busy overnight as the harvesting started.

Hops and the people who picked them are infamous in Kent railway circles. The planning of the trains to bring the pickers from the London area to the hop fields was like a military campaign. Special Control arrangements were established at Paddock Wood, and the branch lines to Hawkhurst and up the Medway Valley suddenly became extremely busy. Many old carriages were retained in sidings round the London suburbs all year long for the 'Hop Pickers' Friends' trains running at weekends so that East End families could visit their menfolk who were working in the hop fields. Frequently whole families stayed in the hop gardens as their annual holiday, all joining in with the work. The trains therefore needed to accommodate their personal effects, usually extensive including such items as sacks of clothing and food, baby carriages, and of course crates of beer.

Special pamphlets containing details of the operation of these services were issued every year to all the stations affected. Elderly locomotives were also dragged out of store and put on the hopping trains.

It is against the background of this intense service that sometimes things could go wrong.

The Accidents

The following are examples of accidents that occurred on the South Eastern Division during the period under review. Most include pictures taken after the event of the damage and clearing-up operations. The descriptions have been condensed from reports of the inquiry by the railway authorities, usually known a 'Joint Enquiries', and from official reports of investigations by the officers of the Ministry of Transport. Occasionally reference is made to newspaper reports.

All the photographs in the following pages are British Railways official views from the late Denis Cullum collection, now in the care of the author, unless otherwise stated.

This view is looking west towards Abbey Wood, with the gypsy camp just visible to the right. (The view eastwards from the crossing towards Plumstead was of equally straight track.) This camp caused the Southern Railway considerable difficulty with misuse of this and other adjacent level crossings on the marshes hereabouts. In the 1953 floods this entire area was inundated, and the gypsies were made homeless; they did not return to the site afterwards. The area is now covered with modern housing and industry as part of Thamesmead new town. Notice the straight approach to the crossing and, on the right, the longitudinal board, which is the rear of the 'Whistle' sign.

Abbey Wood, Boarer's Manor Way

Collision between a train and a road motor vehicle at a level crossing, 24 April 1950

At 5:28pm on 24 April 1950 the 5.21pm up electric passenger train from Slades* Green to Cannon Street, travelling at 45mph, collided with a Bedford 2-ton motor lorry on the level crossing at Boarer's Manor Way between Belvedere and Abbey Wood. At the same moment the 5.09pm Cannon Street to Gillingham was also approaching on the down line, but the driver managed to apply the brakes and avoided a further collision. There were three adults and a babe-in-arms in the lorry cab. All received multiple injuries from which regrettably the baby died.

Boarer's Manor Way was a 'User Worked (Occupation) Crossing', which had gates that closed the road, and opened

* Note that the station at Slades Green was renamed Slade Green from the 1954 Working Timetable onwards to reflect the locals' name for the area.

This is part of the north-side gate at the crossing, which was typical of most Southern user-worked crossings. It has the usual array of notices; those in cast iron include the statutory notice just visible through the gate at the far side, and 'Warning: Stop Look & Listen before crossing the line' signs adjacent to both wickets. This is reinforced by a painted 'Beware of the Trains' sign mostly hidden by the concrete fence post. £2 may seem like a paltry penalty for failing to shut the gate by today's standards, but in 1950 it was a considerable sum. However, today Network Rail threatens a £1,000 fine for similar transgressions.

away from the railway. There were a full set of notices at the crossing at both sides:

1) A statutory warning sign for users of occupation crossings
2) 'Stop Look and Listen'
3) 'Beware of Trains'
4) A conductor rail warning
5) 'Keep the gate shut, penalty 40/-'

It would be known today by Network Rail as a 'bad actor' in that there was a constant history of misuse. The main users were referred to as 'gypsies' (today referred to as 'travellers') who had a semi-permanent encampment on the marshes close to the railway. The gates were persistently left open, and locks and devices associated with the safe working of the gates were damaged or stolen as soon as they were installed.

The Inspecting Officer referred to eighteen previous accidents at this crossing in the preceding twenty-four years, twelve of which had been fatal. The Southern Railway records list only seventeen separate accidents (set out below). Train drivers regarded the crossing as extremely dangerous.

The train driver's evidence was that he had sounded his whistle for a long period as he approached and passed the whistle board 155 yards from the crossing; it was usual for drivers to be cautious here because of the crossing's bad reputation. The lorry appeared to cross the line and enter his path when he was 50 yards from the crossing, and he was powerless to avoid the collision. He released the 'dead man's

handle' (the effect of which was to immediately apply the emergency brake) and took shelter in the cab until after the collision.

The conclusion was that the driver of the lorry had driven on to the crossing without ensuring that it was safe to do so. One of the occupants of the vehicle had got down to open the nearer, down-side gate, this one being the only one closed when the lorry arrived. This person stated that he did not see an approaching train. Another factor may have been the poor visibility, with drizzle reducing visibility to 400 yards.

The known previous history of incidents at the same crossing in brief was:

22 April 1929 – a 68-year-old man was run down and killed by the 12.45 Sheerness to Cannon Street train.

4 September 1929 – a 61-year-old woman was run down and killed by the 11.18am Cannon Street to Dartford train.

11 February 1932 – a 69-year-old man was run down and killed by the 1.07pm Gravesend Central to Cannon Street train.

13 August 1932 – a horse that had gained the line through open gates was electrocuted and subsequently run over by a light locomotive.

25 August 1932 – a contractor's workman carrying a plank was knocked down and injured when a down train struck the plank.

14 January 1933 – a horse-drawn van was struck and damaged by the 3.56pm Charing Cross to Gravesend train.

22 February 1934 – a horse-drawn cart was struck and damaged by the 6.46am Ramsgate to Cannon Street train, and the cart owner who was walking behind it was also killed. The driver of the cart was injured but the carthorse escaped injury.

4 July 1935 – a 39-year-old woman was run down and killed by the 10.25pm Dartford to Charing Cross train.

10 December 1938 – the body of a 68-year-old woman was found at 5.25pm run down and killed, possibly by the 4.43pm Cannon Street to Dartford train.

31 December 1938 – a 55-year-old man was run down and killed by the 8.55pm Charing Cross to Dartford train.

23 November 1939 – a motorcycle was struck by the 4.51pm Slades Green to Cannon Street train, injuring the male rider.

16 January 1941 – a 72-year-old man was run down and killed by the 1.45pm Cannon Street to Gravesend Central train.

7 July 1941 – the 8.08am Cannon Street to Dartford service collided with a cart, injuring the cart driver.

12 August 1941 – the 9.21am Cannon Street to Dartford train struck a motorcycle combination killing the rider and passenger, who were RAF personnel.

7 October 1944 – the 4.18pm Charing Cross to Gillingham train collided with a 2-ton Ford motor lorry, injuring one of the occupants.

20 November 1944 – the 10.51am Dartford to Charing Cross train collided with a 2½-ton motor lorry, wrecking it but not resulting in injuries.

3 July 1949 – an 84-year-old man was run down and killed by the 1.31pm Dartford to Cannon Street train.

Despite the Inspecting Officer making a recommendation that the crossing be abolished, and the Southern Region developing a plan to divert the access to enable the crossing to be closed, which it embarked upon immediately, the proposal fell foul of the entrenched and archaic laws of the land. Erith Borough Council immediately raised objections to the diversion of the right of way, and the matter was still unresolved many years later. In fact, it was not until the wholesale redevelopment of the Erith marshes in the 1960s, which created the new town of Thamesmead, that this crossing was eventually closed on 3 December 1969.

Other user-worked crossings on this particular stretch of railway noted in 1941 included:

Abbey Wood to Belvedere

Buckles Farm	11 miles 71 chains
No 11 Boarer's Manor Way	12 miles 25 chains
Cinder Path/Crossness footpath	12 miles 44 chains
No 13 Leather Bottle	12 miles 44 chains

For completeness, the railway-operated or attended level crossings were located at:

Abbey Wood to Belvedere

Abbey Wood/Harrow Manor Way	11 miles 49 chains

Belvedere to Erith

Belvedere station	12 miles 75 chains
Picardy Manor Way	13 miles 9 chains
Crabtree Manor Way	13 miles 22 chains
Pembroke Road	13 miles 63 chains

This busy route was hampered by the terrain, which was marshy ground flat and level with the formation on both sides of the line. All the level crossings were eventually eliminated by bridges built over the line or by diversion, but it was only in the 1970s with the Dartford area resignalling that this was eventually achieved.

Borough Market Junction

Derailment of a passenger train, 12 August 1958

At 7.30am on Tuesday 12 August 1958 the 6.52am up electric passenger train from Sanderstead to Cannon Street became derailed on Borough Market Junction's No 26 facing points in the up local line.

The train concerned was formed of ten coaches, with two 4EPB units leading and a 2EPB unit coupled to the rear. The derailment occurred at the points where the Charing Cross up line diverged to the left from the up Cannon Street local line.

The eighth vehicle of the train was the first to leave the rails, when the motor bogie of Driving Motor Second coach No S14062S of unit No 5031 came off the track, and was sheared from under the carriage. The leading bogie would have been travelling correctly towards Cannon Street, but the motor bogie was on the up local towards Charing Cross. The bodywork of No S14062S then struck the bridge parapet, throwing it sideways, causing the loss of the motor bogie and subsequent derailment of the leading bogie also. It was also foul of the up through line, as was the ninth vehicle.

The ninth vehicle (Driving Trailer Second No S77550 of unit No 5751), which became detached from the eighth vehicle, was also derailed and slewed across the up local to Cannon Street and the down Charing Cross and up Charing Cross lines, losing its second bogie in the process, but the last vehicle remained on the track. The displacement of the conductor rail

The motor bogie from 4EPB No 5031, torn off in the derailment, lies across the down Charing Cross line at Borough Market Junction on 12 August 1958. The bridge parapet has been damaged and the remains of one of the wooden shoe beams with the collector shoe still attached is impaled on one end of it. This area has recently been extensively remodelled to remove the two-track bottleneck in connection with the expansion of Thameslink services.

caused a short-circuit and cut off current to all lines. With all up lines to Charing Cross and Cannon Street obstructed, the up peak-hour service was curtailed at London Bridge. The Cannon Street services were resumed in time for the evening peak, but full normal operation to Charing Cross did not resume until late that evening.

Being quite early in the day, the rear of the train was not heavily loaded and casualties were light. Six passengers complained of minor injuries and were treated but not detained.

Investigation revealed that the derailment was caused by excessive wear, known as 'side cutting', of the left-hand point switch, which had caused the wheel of the train to ride up on to the top of the rail head, and subsequently fall off the wrong side of the rail. The wear on the switches had been inspected by the ganger two days earlier and reported on the Monday morning. The Permanent Way Inspector had also inspected the rail on Sunday, so was aware of the problem. However, the

conclusion he came to was that the wear was no more severe than that at other points in his area, and that they only needed replacement within nine months.

The track in this area was some of the most heavily used in the world: 210 trains passed over No 26 points towards Charing Cross and an additional sixty-five trains passed towards Cannon Street every weekday. This factor meant that track inspections, maintenance and renewal were difficult to schedule and could only be considered for weekends when traffic was lighter. The switches in 95lb bullhead rail were 'E' type curved switches with joggled stock rails, which allowed a 3/8-inch switch toe. The stock rail is the rail against which the switch blade presses to turnout, but otherwise provided a route through the points.

Because of high wear the rails here were specified to be of manganese steel, which had better wear resistance than carbon steel, but also resulted in longer delivery times when renewal was required. The switches had indeed been replaced

Above: **The Driving Trailer Second of 2EPB No 5751 lies across both up and down Charing Cross lines at Borough Market Junction as the permanent way and breakdown gangs decide how they are going to clear up the mess. From the expressions, the presence of the photographer was not appreciated!**

Left: **The rearmost Motor Brake Second of 4EPB No 5031 is derailed all wheels, but the rest of the train is properly on the track. The train is standing on the up Cannon Street through line. The derailed trailing bogie is actually sitting over bridge No 45 (Borough Market), which is distinguished by the transition from ballasted sleepered track on top of brick arches to rails supported by wheel timbers on the steel-decked bridge. Despite the damage to No S14062S, it was repaired and eventually added to unit No 5021, replacing No S14041S, which was damaged beyond economic repair at Crayford Creek Junction on 17 February 1959. It was in turn replaced in No 5031 by No S14046S from unit No 5023, which was disbanded following the Maze Hill collision on 4 July 1958.**

Above: **The other side of Driving Trailer Second No S77550 of 2EPB No 5751. The inner bogie of this vehicle has also been torn off and is lying to one side. Note, too, the winch attached to the rail with wire rope. This manual device has now been superseded by hydraulic lifting and pulling gear, but illustrates the strenuous effort needed by breakdown gangs to clear up the wreckage after a railway accident. Unit No 5751 was eventually repaired and returned to traffic.**

Right: **The offending ill-fitting switch rail of Borough Market Junction No 26 points is seen here. The S&T Department point fitters appear to have moved out of the way for the photograph, and have left their tools awaiting their return. This photograph also illustrates just how greasy and slippery the track, especially the sleepers, can become.**

Left: The driving cab end of unit No 5031's rear motor coach No S14062S now lies on the rails, having had its motor bogie torn from under it by contact with the end of the bridge parapet girder.

Below: The bogie from No 5031 lies in the foreground and Driving Trailer Second No S77550 of 2EPB unit No 5751 lies to one side. The railway officers, distinguished by their suits and homburg hats, are distinctly identifiable from the breakdown gang in overalls, and are present to gather information and decide what should be done next. One wonders what point was being emphasised with the umbrella! (The accident enquiry was conducted by Col W. P. Reed. Despite extensive searching, no image of Col Reed has come to light and it might therefore be suspected that he could well be one of the officials seen here.)

on 15 March that year but, because manganese steel switches had not been available, carbon steel switches and stock rail had been installed instead. These had worn rapidly, more than expected, and in fact the side cut wear of the left-hand stock rail had completely removed the 'joggle'. The left-hand switch toe of the points towards Cannon Street was in fact protruding and created a 'ramp' to deflect the wheel flange to ride up on top of the rail.

The ganger had inspected the points on the previous Sunday and found a 2-inch-long sliver of metal broken from the top of the switch rail; he reported to his Inspector on Monday that it should be changed. The Inspector, having himself also inspected the points, decided to undertake the replacement on the following weekend. He failed to realise that the switches were carbon steel, not manganese steel, and thus susceptible to more rapid wear, and was less concerned about the immediacy of the problem.

The Ministry of Transport Inspecting officer holding the inquiry considered this to be an error of judgement on the part of the Permanent Way Inspector, letting his previous experience override the view of changed circumstances. Between 1947 and 1950 manganese steel switches were returning life spans of 22 months, but since 1952 the life had decreased progressively to nine months in 1957. Carbon steel had been used intermittently and needed to be replaced at about 60% of the life expectancy of manganese steel. The problem had become worse since ten-car electric and twelve-car diesel working had been introduced, with wear rates increasing significantly, and it was to be hoped that BR Southern Region would learn from this accident.

Borough Market Junction

Collision between passenger trains, 28 January 1960

This accident featured in the previous edition of 'The Other Side of the Southern', but additional information and pictures have been taken from the internal Joint Inquiry report, so it is thought appropriate to include it here.

On Thursday 28 January 1960 at 2.58pm a triple collision occurred at Borough Market Junction. The 1.00pm diesel multiple unit train (unit No 1014) from Hastings to Charing Cross was passing the junction on the up local line when the 2.22pm Hayes to Charing Cross train passed Borough Market's No D19 signal at danger and crossed into the path of the Hastings train, which collided with the leading carriage of the

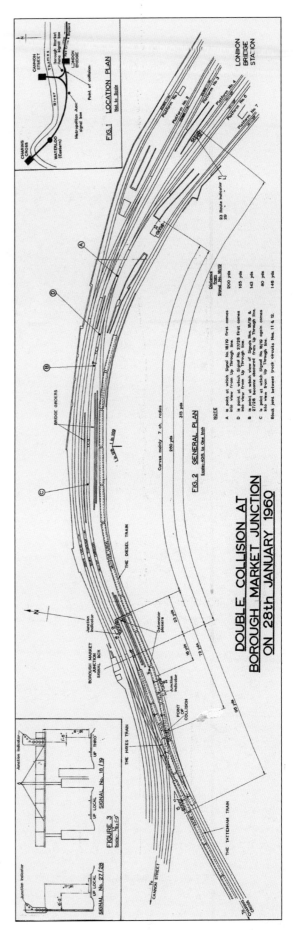

Borough Market Junction: accident plan, 28 January 1960. *Ministry of Transport, Crown Copyright Reserved*

Overleaf left: **Driving Motor Brake Second No S60021 of DEMU 6L unit No 1014 leans precariously towards the parapet of the viaduct and close to one of the adjacent buildings that line the track hereabouts.**

Right: **After the rear three carriages of the Hayes train had been drawn back clear, the leading motor coach of the Hastings train still rests precariously against the leading motor coach.**

Dealt with previously in Special No 8 'The Other Side of the Southern', a few more photographs taken on the night shift are to hand and may help to identify some of the rolling stock involved. The Hastings service was being led by DEMU unit No 1014, Driving Motor Brake Second No 60021 leading, and the Hayes service by 4EPB unit No 5169. No S15390S was formed into 4EPB No S5212 at that time.

Hayes train. The first and second carriages of the Hayes train (unit No 5169) became derailed and forced foul of the down Charing Cross line just as the 2.53pm Charing Cross to Tattenham Corner train (unit No 5212) was about to pass. With insufficient time to stop, this train then struck the derailed carriages of the Hayes train. The leading carriage of the Hastings train was derailed towards the parapet of the bridge, and the second carriage was in contact with the third carriage of the Hayes train.

Fortunately the collision occurred at slow speed, both trains running virtually neck and neck from London Bridge station. However, the diesel train was running under clear signals and passed London Bridge station non-stop as booked on the up local line; meanwhile the electric train was receiving restrictive aspects on the up through line, and at Borough Market Junction No D18 signal, protecting the junction, was at danger to allow the diesel train to proceed towards Waterloo.

There were about 115 passengers in the diesel train, twenty-five passengers in the Hayes train, and ninety-eight passengers in the Tattenham train. Seven passengers, most of whom were in the Hayes train, received slight injuries or suffered from shock. One passenger was sent to hospital but was discharged after treatment, while the remainder were given first aid treatment, then continued on their journeys.

Borough Market Junction is the point where the four-track route from London Bridge diverged to Cannon Street and to Waterloo (Eastern) and Charing Cross. It was a most important

junction and the traffic through it was extremely heavy. The junction was mainly on viaducts.

In the up direction from London Bridge the lines ran generally westwards and were mainly on sharp left-handed curves to Borough Market Junction signal box, which was about 260 yards beyond the platforms. The four-track route to Cannon Street then took a sharp right-handed curve to the north, while the double-track route to Charing Cross continued westwards for a short distance before swinging to the left. The up lines rose at 1 in 109 through London Bridge to a point roughly halfway between the platforms and the signal box, then fell at 1 in 128 through the junction. Metropolitan Junction was the next box towards Charing Cross.

On account of the severe curvature, the speed of trains through Borough Market Junction was restricted to 20mph

The signalling installation at Borough Market Junction was brought into use in 1928. The signals were of the four-aspect colour light type and were closely spaced. They and the electrically operated points were controlled from a miniature 35-lever power frame in Borough Market Junction signal box. On the up local line the signals concerned in this case were D35, the starter from No 7 Platform, and D27/28, which was situated at the diverging junction on that line and was 276 yards beyond D35. On the up through line the starting signal from No 4 Platform was D23/29, which was equipped with a 'theatre'-type route indicator; it was 55 yards east of signal D35. Signal D23, with the letter 'T' on the route indicator, led over the up through line to signal D18/19. The latter signal was situated at the diverging junction on that line, and was 292 yards beyond D23. (Signal No D27/28 was in fact one signal which had a right-handed lunar light junction indicator, and was controlled by two levers. It was referred to as signal D27 when, having been cleared by lever 27, it controlled the route to Cannon Street with the junction indicator illuminated, and as signal D28 when, having been cleared by lever No 28, it controlled the route to Charing Cross without the indicator being illuminated Similarly, signal D18 with the indicator illuminated led to Cannon Street and signal D19, without the indicator, to Charing Cross.)

Signals D28 and D19 were also controlled electrically from Metropolitan Junction box and neither could be cleared until a slot lever in that box had been reversed. The slot lever released either signal lever in the Borough Market Junction frame for one train movement only, but the usual mechanical locking in the frame prevented the two signal levers from being reversed simultaneously. The reversal of the slot lever was indicated in Borough Market Junction box. When the slot was being given and lever No 28 or No 19 had been reversed, the aspect of the signal concerned would clear to yellow, double yellow or green depending on the aspect of the next signal(s) ahead at Metropolitan Junction. When signal D23 was yellow, the aspect in signal D19 was red.

On account of the slow speed of trains, the overlaps beyond signals were short. The overlap beyond signal D19 was only 59 yards, and in the case of some other signals it was considerably less.

The area was continuously track-circuited and the track circuits exercised the usual controls over the signals and points. When a signal was being cleared it was 'approach locked' by the occupation by a train of the berth track circuit, but the lever could be placed in the 'back-lock' position, which replaced the aspect of the signal to red. The locking was released when a track circuit ahead of the signal was occupied and the signal lever had been replaced to normal. In the case of signal D19, the berth track circuit was No 12, which began 146 yards on the approach side of the signal. The track circuit next ahead of the signal was No 13, and when it was occupied the aspect of the signal was replaced to red. However, in the case of signal D28, the aspect was replaced to red by the occupation of the second track circuit ahead of the signal, i.e. No 17.

The signal box was provided with an illuminated diagram on which the occupation of the track circuits was shown by lights. The aspects of the signals were repeated separately by coloured lights situated above the respective levers in the frame. There were no block instruments and trains were signalled by block bells and describers.

'Train ready to start' plungers were provided on each platform at London Bridge and, when operated, they provided visual indications in Borough Market Junction box.

Mechanically operated detonator placers were provided, worked by separate levers in the box. On the up local and up through lines they were almost opposite signals D27/28 and D18/19 respectively.

In this photograph taken during the night, probably shortly before the withdrawal of the non-derailed coaches of the Hayes train, thus removing the photographer's vantage point, the identity of the leading unit of the Tattenham train can clearly be made out.

Signal D18/19 could first be seen by the driver of a train on the up through line at a distance of 200 yards to the left of a bridge girder between the up through and the up local lines; it remained in view for 57 yards till it was then obscured by the bridge girder. It again came into view beyond the girder at a distance of 80 yards and remained in view until it was reached. The signal was focussed towards the furthest point and consequently its light aspect was not brilliant when seen on closer approach.

The guard of a four-coach electric train on the up through line could get only a momentary view of this signal before its aspect, if at clear, was changed to red by the train occupying the track circuit ahead of it.

Signal D27/28 came into the view of a driver of a train on the up local line at a distance of 184 yards.

It could also be seen by a driver of a train on the up through line at a distance of 165 yards from signal D18/19. It remained in view for a distance of about 22 yards and was then obscured by the bridge girder, after which it again came into view. Signal D27/28 was focussed towards the up local line and its aspects were not brilliant when seen from the up through line. A train on the up local line a coach length or more ahead of the train on the up through line does, however, obstruct the view of this signal from a train on the up through line.

When the two signals were both in view, D27/28 was considerably to the left of and less brilliant than D18/19.

The investigation concluded that the signalling had operated correctly, and that signal D18/19 had remained at red as the Hayes train approached it. The driver of the Hayes train was therefore responsible for passing the signal at danger. Colonel McMullen recommended that extra co-acting detonator placers should be considered for signals at Borough Market Junction. He also recommended extending the approach track locking to bring it in line with modern practice.

Left: **Coach No S14423S is the Driving Motor Brake Second of 4EPB Set No 5212, which was the leading unit of the Tattenham Corner train. Seen here is the damage caused by striking the second coach of the already derailed train from Hayes to Charing Cross.**

Cannon Street

Collision between a light engine and a passenger train, 21 February 1949

At 5.17pm a steam locomotive, 'O1' Class No 1425, running light under clear signals from Platform 7, collided with the 4.58pm Bromley North to Cannon Street train on the up local line. It was determined at the inquiry that the motorman had passed signals C36 and C28/C34 at red and run through 27 points.

The electric train was formed of two four-car suburban units, No 4483 leading and No 4121. Motor coach No 8379 of unit No 4483 was derailed by the leading bogie and sustained damage to the driving compartment, and locomotive No 1425 sustained minor damage. No injuries were reported.

The motorman appears to have read the through line signals as applying to himself.

The circumstance of this accident was repeated on 9 April 1951, which follows.

Cannon Street

Collision between electric passenger trains, 9 April 1951

At 8.59am on Monday 9 April 1951 the 8.22am Sevenoaks to Cannon Street electric passenger train came into head-on collision with the 8.58am Cannon Street to Charing Cross electric train in the vicinity of 93 points. The cause was attributed to the motorman of the Sevenoaks train failing to stop at Cannon Street's C36 and C28/C24 signals on the up local line, which were at red, and running through 27 points. At the same time as the 8.22am from Sevenoaks was approaching Cannon Street, the motorman was driving the 8.22am Orpington to Cannon Street correctly under clear signals on the up through line towards Platform 1. He was about to pass the train on the up local line, which had come to a stand just ahead, when he saw a motorman on the track waving and immediately brought his train to a stand, and observed that the train on the up local had been in collision with another train. The motorman of the 8.58am Cannon Street to Charing Cross, formed from the 8.30am Bromley North to Cannon Street, had departed from Platform 5 under a yellow aspect signal with route indicator 'B', preparing to be directed right towards Metropolitan Junction, when he saw another train approaching on the same line. He made an emergency brake application, then jumped from the cab when they were 10 yards apart. He touched the conductor rail and received a slight shock. He then waved down the approaching Orpington train, before climbing back into the cab to attend to the motorman of the Sevenoaks train, who was

Cannon Street, 9 April 1951.

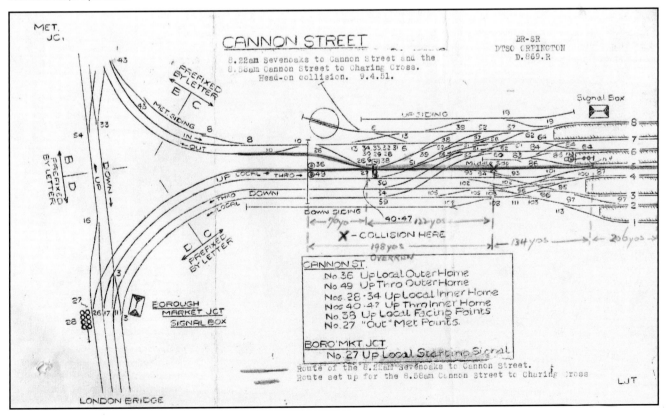

Driving Motor Brake Thirds Nos S8146 (down train) and S8828 (up train) are here seen impacted into each other following a signal passed at danger outside Cannon Street station. No S8146 was part of 4SUB unit No 4309. (This was originally three-car suburban unit No 1294, built new in 1925 for the extension of the LSWR electrification by the Southern Railway. This was a batch of units on a non-standard 59ft 6in underframe instead of the standard 62ft 6in underframes that the Southern used for practically all of its suburban electric fleet.) Despite its age and the damage sustained, unit No 4309, including coach No S8146S, was repaired and survived until 1960. No S8828 also soldiered on after the accident in unit No 4244 until 1953, when it gave up its underframe for new 4EPB Motor Brake Third No S140921S.

This is a closer view of the guard's van and bogie of No S8146. The Maunsell carriage stock styling of these few new-build electric multiple units contrasts with the hotchpotch of body styles of the reconstructed former LSWR, LBSCR and SER suburban carriages that were used for the majority of the pre-war electric suburban fleet.

Opposite top: **The force in a relatively low-speed impact can still do considerable damage, as testified by the bent buffer-head of No S8828.**

Opposite bottom: **Some detail of the motor bogie is included, which also shows the severed current lead from the shoe beam. The traction motor on the rear axle may also be noted.**

trapped in his cab. Six passengers in the Sevenoaks train and the motorman were injured, none seriously.

At the inquiry the motorman of the Sevenoaks train accepted that he must have been reading the signals meant for the Orpington train on the up through line, and not those for the up local, which were indeed his signals. The guard of the Sevenoaks train also maintained that he was reading clear signals as they passed Borough Market Junction, but a thorough test by the Signal & Telegraph Engineer proved beyond doubt that the signalling equipment was working correctly.

The trains were both composed of eight carriages. The 8.22am from Sevenoaks was formed of units Nos 4244 (S8828, S9342, S9244, S8214) and 4603 (S12657, S10287, S10297, S12654), and the 8.58am from Cannon Street was formed of units Nos 4309 (S8146, S9444, S10369, S8145) and 4228 (S8045, S9210, S9358, S8005).

Damage occurred as follows:

S8828 – cab very extensively damaged, two solebars bent, one headstock bent, two buffer rods bent, 'view' glasses in compartments 'C', 'E' and 'F' broken, all front jumpers and cab controls damaged

S12657 – headstock trailing end offside slightly bent

S12654 – headstock leading end nearside slightly bent

S8146 – body overrode No S8828 by approximately 5ft 9in. Leading bogie forced out of position by 18 inches, and trailing wheels of leading bogie derailed. Centre pin bent, one headstock bent, one bogie frame headstock bent, two buffer rods bent, two buffer castings broken,

floor of guard's compartment damaged, end panel of driving cab slightly damaged, brake hoses damaged, motor and shoe leads damaged, reverser damaged, No 2 motor junction box damaged

S10369 – headstock leading end nearside slightly bent

No 27 points – run through by the 8.22am from Sevenoaks and two switch rails and drive rods damaged

Recovery was completed by 2.30pm, but delays and cancellations to other services were extensive, and lasted well into the afternoon.

Cannon Street

Signal passed at danger and collision, 20 March 1961

At about 9.15am on 20 March 1961 Cannon Street became the scene of yet another accident. The 8.33am up electric passenger train from Addiscombe to Cannon Street, consisting of six coaches filled with passengers, ran by C89, the up through home and C81/C88 up through starting signals of Cannon Street signal box at danger, and collided at between 10 and 15mph with the 9.14am twelve-coach empty diesel-electric train from Cannon Street to Grove Park, which was travelling at about the same speed under clear signals from No 6 Platform across the route of the up train to the down local line.

Cannon Street, 20 April 1961.
Ministry of Transport, Crown Copyright Reserved

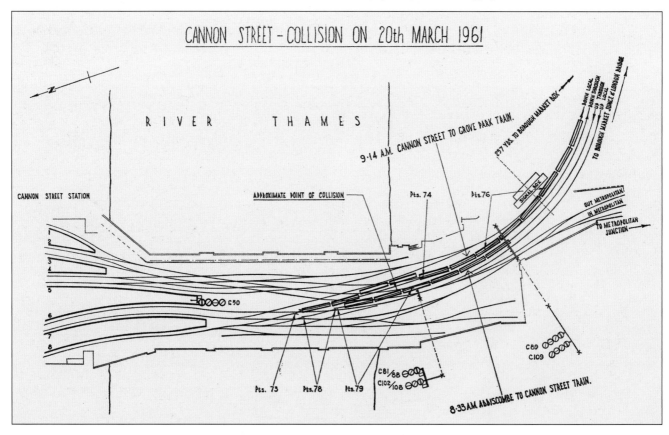

Trailer Corridor Second No S60542 of 6L DEMU No 1014 is partially tilted and shows signs of the side scrape with the Driving Motor Brake Second of 4EPB No S5225. No S60542 was the eighth coach of the twelve-coach diesel empty stock train, and the first vehicle to be struck. Motor Brake Second No S60028, which was the seventh vehicle, remains upright. The leading six-car set was unscathed and removed from the scene as soon as practicable. Unfortunately the next two carriages (Nos S60543 and S60714) of the diesel train were completely on their sides. Note in the background a train of 4CEP stock being hauled away from Cannon Street and the derailed trains by two BR Sulzer Type 2 diesel-electric locomotives in charge; this train from Ramsgate was approaching the scene when the collision occurred but stopped just in time to avoid hitting it. It was necessary to use locomotives to remove the coaches because all traction current had been discharged when the collision occurred, and was isolated for safety purposes. There is also a clear view of the fairly new Cannon Street 'C' signal cabin, which was erected after the disastrous fire in the original cabin in 1957.

Left: **Driving Motor Brake Second No S14449S of 4EPB No 5225 shows the damage to the 'fireman's' side caused by the collision. The older style of large roller blind numerals is clearly visible.**

Below: **Trailer Corridor First No S60714 of unit No 1014 is seen here in the sidings at Cannon Street after re-railing. This vehicle was not the first to be struck in the collision, but ended up completely on its side. The marks of the initial collision are clearly visible. These vehicles were introduced in 1957 and were the only BR Mark 1 passenger-carrying stock built to SR Restriction '0' for working between Tonbridge and Hastings. This same set, No 1014, had also been involved in the accident at Borough Market Junction in 1960.**

No S60543 is on its side with a huge hole punched into it by the cab of No S14449S.

The 8.33am electric train struck the right-hand leading edge and side of the eighth coach of the outgoing diesel train; it also scored the side of this coach, then struck the right-hand leading end of the ninth coach, crushed the body severely, and overturned it and the following coach. The first two coaches of the electric train were derailed to the left and stopped leaning to that side, but there was little damage to their interiors and no passengers were seriously injured. Eleven out of an estimated load of 650 passengers had minor injuries and were taken to hospital, as was the motorman, who suffered from shock. The other passengers were conducted on foot to Cannon Street station without avoidable delay.

An incoming electric passenger train from Ramsgate on the adjacent up local line, also heavily loaded, which was closely following the train from Addiscombe, was stopped by its motorman before coming level with the derailed coaches, from which passengers had begun to detrain; its passengers were also conducted to the station.

There was a delay of a few minutes before all tracks in the area of the accident were isolated from the electric current, but there were no casualties on this account.

Three of the four lines between London Bridge and Cannon Street were blocked by the collision and it was necessary to close the fourth line, at first for the safe conduct of the passengers, then for the removal of the derailed stock. The in and out lines between Cannon Street and Metropolitan Junction were also closed for a time to facilitate the clearance of the rolling stock. Cannon Street was therefore closed to traffic during the day and evening, and trains were diverted to, and were started from, other South London termini. All lines were cleared and normal services were resumed at 4.47am on the following morning.

Let us first look at the location where this occurred. Cannon Street is on the north bank of the River Thames and all routes from it go south over the river before diverging eastwards towards London Bridge station; there are also connections to the lines to Blackfriars and Charing Cross via Metropolitan Junction. Following the 'ten-car scheme' works in 1956, the station was extended onto the bridge. The junction at the station throat was all on the bridge. The track is severely curved as it threads its way over the surrounding streets. The four tracks towards London Bridge are on a sharp curve of 10 chains radius, decreasing to 7 chains at the new Cannon Street signal box. The gradient towards Borough Market Junction is rising at 1 in 150. There is a permanent speed restriction of 20mph on all lines.

The routes were all signalled by four-aspect colour lights operated from Cannon Street or Borough Market Junction signal boxes. Cannon Street signal box was barely four years old, having replaced one destroyed by fire in 1957 and a temporary signal box in use for a short time after that. Signals were located on gantries above the appropriate tracks. The trains concerned were running side by side on the up through and up local lines.

The damaged and derailed coaches of both trains await re-railing and clearing up. In the distance are the carriages of the Ramsgate to Cannon Street express, which stopped before the derailment, and which appears to have been worked subsequently past the site into the station, presumably to aid the recovery. The locomotives used for this shunt are to be seen in an earlier photograph.

The electric train from Addiscombe comprised a four-coach unit and a two-coach unit, having a total weight of 206 tons and a length of 130 yards. It had started that morning as a ten-coach train, but a hot axle box had made it necessary to detach a four-coach unit at Addiscombe. It was fitted with the Westinghouse brake with electro-pneumatic operation on all wheels with a brake power of 85 per cent on the motor bogies and 75 per cent on the trailer bogies. The buckeye coupling was in use between the two units, and the three-link intermediate close coupling between the coaches of each unit. The coaches were of all-steel construction except for the floors, which were of wood.

The diesel-electric train comprised two six-coach units of a total weight of 462 tons and a length of 265 yards. It had the buckeye coupling throughout and the same type of brakes as the electric train. It was also of all-steel construction.

There was only minor damage to the track and much of the damage to the trains will be seen in the pictures.

The driver of the Addiscombe train stated that he saw signal C89 at single yellow, but tests of the signalling demonstrated that the signal would have been held at red by the interlocking. He also believed that he saw C81 clear from red to a green with an '8' route indication. However, a passenger on the train who was looking out confirmed in evidence that both these signals were red and remained so. It is possible that the driver of the Addiscombe train read across to the signals on the parallel up local line, which were showing 'proceed' aspects for the approaching train from Ramsgate (C109 and C102/C108).

The Inspecting Officer concluded that the home and starting signals on the up through line were properly at danger as the 8.33am up electric passenger train from Addiscombe approached them, and that they remained at danger as the train passed them. The responsibility for the accident therefore rested on the motorman of that train. The view of the signals was a short one because of the sharp curvature, but speeds were low and drivers had no real difficulty in identifying them.

The Inspector leading the inquiry considered the use of co-acting detonators at the signals concerned, but left the matter to British Railways to decide; a similar decision was come to with reference to the British Railways automatic warning system of train control (AWS). However, he did acknowledge that the Southern Region priority for the installation of the automatic warning system has been given to the higher-speed routes to the West, and the system had not yet been applied to the electrified lines, which were equipped for the most part with colour light signals; he did not think that any change should be made in the priorities.

Catford

Derailment of a passenger train at 2.25pm, 23 September 1946

The 2.10pm express passenger train from Victoria to Ramsgate became derailed at about 35mph approaching Catford station, with most of the carriages falling down the embankment into the car park of Catford Greyhound Stadium.

Unfortunately one passenger was killed and sixteen injured, requiring hospital treatment. Forty-five passengers sustained minor injuries or complained of shock. The seating capacity of the train was 432, with 377 of them occupied.

The train was hauled by Class 'V' 'Schools' Class 4-4-0 No 917 *Ardingly*, and was composed of nine bogie carriages. From the engine these were Nos TK 801 (loose), and set 460 formed of BTK 3563, TKs 977 and 991, CKs 5508, 5507, 5506 and 5505, and BTK 3562. All coaches in set 460 were the 'Restriction 1' 'Thanet' stock, screw-coupled with British Standard gangways.

The locomotive left the rails at 7 miles 63 chains and 4 yards from Victoria, running derailed for 273 yards until coming to rest still upright on the track, but with all wheels derailed. It stopped 80 yards from Catford station platform.

Damage to the locomotive consisted of steps and sand gear bent and broken. The tender sustained considerable damage, including sand pipes bent and broken, steps bent, right-hand trailing axle box broken and horn sheet bent, left leading and middle axle journals burred, brake reservoir broken, back buffer beam pierced by a rail, and brake gear damaged.

The carriages suffered severe damage, as follows:

TK 801 – derailed at right angles leaning towards the falling embankment, heavily damaged and broken up on site. A rail penetrated the gangway door and reappeared halfway along the carriage body.

BTK 3563 – derailed and down the embankment, heavily damaged and broken up on site.

TK 977 – derailed and at the foot of the embankment, heavily damaged and broken up on site.

TK 991 – derailed and leaning down the embankment, heavily damaged and broken up on site.

CK 5508 – solebar slightly bent, wheels bruised, axle box liner broken, one side spring hanger bent, one

Catford, 20 September 1946.
Southern Railway, Cullum collection

'V' Class 'Schools' No 917 *Ardingly* is derailed at Catford on 20 September 1946. Duty number 478 displayed on the headcode disc was a Ramsgate locomotive duty, but the driver and fireman were Faversham men who had worked up to London with the same locomotive earlier in that day. No 917 had run 48,000 miles since its last General Overhaul; however, the inspection after the derailment revealed no defects that might have contributed to the accident. *S. C. Townroe, Rod Blencowe collection*

The buffer beam of the tender of No 917 was pierced by a displaced conductor rail from the down line. There was considerable damage to the tender steps, sand pipes and brake equipment, and one axle box was broken by the force of the derailment. The brick parapets belonging to bridge No 469 'Recreation Ground C' were fortunately not damaged. The matchwood to be seen underneath the tender is the remains of some of the 288 sleepers destroyed in the derailment.
S. C. Townroe, Rod Blencowe collection

The first carriage of the 2.10pm Victoria to Ramsgate train, Corridor Third No 801, has come to rest on the retaining wall, and the second vehicle, Corridor Third Brake No 3563, has landed in the car park of Catford Greyhound Stadium, with the guard's compartment completely demolished. These two vehicles were broken up on site, and the following two carriages, Corridor Thirds Nos 977 and 991, were also scrapped as a result of damage sustained. The single fatality was to a passenger travelling in No 801.

Another view of Corridor Third No 801 shows that a rail displaced in the derailment has penetrated the carriage and threaded its way through three compartments. The site was a difficult one for rescue and recovery, being situated on a embankment with retaining wall.

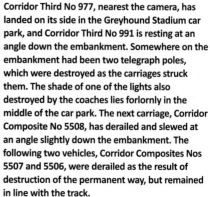

Corridor Third No 977, nearest the camera, has landed on its side in the Greyhound Stadium car park, and Corridor Third No 991 is resting at an angle down the embankment. Somewhere on the embankment had been two telegraph poles, which were destroyed as the carriages struck them. The shade of one of the lights also destroyed by the coaches lies forlornly in the middle of the car park. The next carriage, Corridor Composite No 5508, has derailed and slewed at an angle slightly down the embankment. The following two vehicles, Corridor Composites Nos 5507 and 5506, were derailed as the result of destruction of the permanent way, but remained in line with the track.

The destruction of the permanent way of the down line is graphically illustrated here with the sleepers shredded into matchwood, and rails and chairs scattered. The devastating effect of the displaced rail piercing the end of Corridor Third No 801 is again evident. It has reappeared from the gangway connection, having demolished three compartments and the lavatory. This end of the carriage was in fact the leading end in the direction of travel, and it has been spun round by the force of the derailment. Clearin up has started and a crane is visible in the distance preparing to re-rail locomotive No 917.

gangway damaged, two step irons bent, two top step boards damaged, roof cornices damaged, recovered.

CK 5507 – derailed all wheels, two step irons bent, one side spring eye bolt bent, two solebars slightly bent, recovered.

CK 5506 – derailed one bogie and two wheels of rear bogie.

The other coaches were not derailed.

The down line over twelve complete 60-foot lengths of track were destroyed, and two telephone poles demolished.

The train was being checked to 40mph for a speed restriction that started beyond the point of derailment, and was just passing the Greyhound Stadium when the locomotive rolled badly left and right and the driver, feeling this, applied the vacuum brake. It appears that the leading pair of wheels on the bogie had jumped off the rail and moved to the right,

and this then caused the trailing pair to derail to the left. This disrupted the track and caused the rest of the locomotive and tender wheels to derail, further destroying the permanent way and derailing the coaches behind. One of the rails became displaced and twisted, puncturing the gangway of the leading carriage and the rear of the locomotive tender.

The weather had been wet for a long period, and the track was known to be susceptible to movement in wet conditions. The cant (the height of the outer rail above the inner one on a curve) was found afterwards to be irregular, but this defect had probably existed over a number of days. The wheels of the bogie were probably thrown off by an irregularity, but no defect with the locomotive that could have contributed to this was found. The inquiry considered that the permanent way inspection procedures had been deficient. No blame was attached to the locomotive or the train crew.

Between Charing and Lenham

Derailment of the 9.50pm Ashford to Hither Green freight train, 9 December 1949

At 10.21pm on 9 December 1949 the 9.50pm freight train from Ashford to Hither Green hauled by 'N15' Class 4-6-0 No 30800 became derailed at 51 miles 37 chains between Charing and Lenham, on the Maidstone East line. The cause was determined as a sudden and unpredictable collapse of a portion of the embankment as the weight of the locomotive came on to it. The embankment was being watched following inspections that had revealed a number of weaknesses, and work had been undertaken during the preceding month to tip ashes on to the embankment to stabilise it. A 15mph temporary speed restriction was in force and the BR inquiry concluded that the train was complying with this when the accident occurred.

The train consisted of forty wagons, nine loaded with coal, four of sugar beet, eleven of ordinary goods, fifteen empty wagons and a 25-ton brake van.

During November the local ganger had noticed a deterioration of the embankment and track levels near an old slip site at 51 miles 38 chains, and called the District Permanent Way Inspector, who examined the line the following day. As a result of this inspection, three and a half wagon loads of ash had been ordered and tipped at the site on 29 November, and some fettling had been carried out on the up line to counteract the slippage. This seemed to be having the desired effect, until the situation appears to have become worse on the afternoon of 8 December and the ganger again called the District Permanent Way Inspector's office for permission to put a man on duty at the site to act as a watchman. Permanent way staff had been in attendance from then until the following morning, when the Chief Permanent Way Inspector attended personally and decided that a temporary speed restriction was necessary. As a result a 15mph TSR was imposed from 4.00pm, 'C' and 'T' boards (which mark the commencement and termination of the restriction) were erected, and notices posted in motive power depots from 12.30pm. A flagman (hand-signalman) with detonators was also provided.

Work to fettle the track at the slip site continued, but because of manpower shortages the hand-signalman was withdrawn just after 9.00pm to help with the work, leaving just the freight to pass.

The previous train, the 7.25pm Ramsgate to Holborn Viaduct hauled by an 'E1' Class 4-4-0, passed over the slip site safely at about 9.52pm and on inquiry the driver and the guard both reported a 'lurch', but not sufficient to cause alarm or to cause them to lose balance. The gang working on the track found that the track had dropped half an inch after the passage of the Ramsgate to Holborn service, but had managed to raise the track 7/8 inch and achieve a solid road bed before the freight was due.

The Hither Green driver in charge of No 30800 stated that he was well aware of the temporary speed restriction and controlled his train accordingly. Various checks and corroborative evidence confirmed that the train was running at less than 15mph at the 'C' board.

It appears that the catastrophic slip occurred at the moment the driving wheels were over that spot. This caused the bogie wheels to ride up and derail, and the locomotive ended up on its left side, bringing off the rest of the train and resulting in twenty-four wagons becoming derailed, seventeen becoming damaged beyond economic repair, four severely damaged, and three slightly damaged. The guard suffered facial injuries, but no one else was injured. The footplate crew immediately started to protect the line, the fireman going forward with a red lamp and detonators, while the driver dumped the fire. The permanent way staff telephoned both Charing and Lenham signalmen straight away, who immediately blocked the line. The guard was taken by the PW staff to a nearby road, where a local doctor summoned by them attended to his injuries.

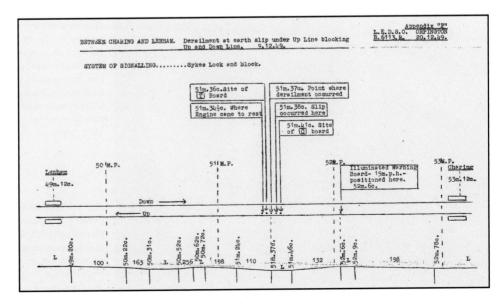

A sketch plan of the accident site.
BR Southern Region, Cullum collection

Above; 'N15' Class 'King Arthur' 4-6-0 No 30800 *Sir Meleaus de Lile* lies derailed all wheels and completely on its side following an earth slip at 51 miles 37 chains, between Charing and Lenham. The entire Ashford-Hither Green goods train was derailed and many of the wagons were so badly damaged that they were broken up on site. No 30800 was one of the final batch of fourteen Maunsell 'Arthurs', built at Eastleigh in 1926 and intended for the Central Section. For this allocation they were supplied with Ashford-pattern 3,500-gallon six-wheel tenders, as seen here, which were lighter and did not exceed the weight restrictions prevalent on the Central Section. These tenders had modified drawgear, making tender swaps difficult, which resulted in Nos 793 to 806 keeping their original tenders throughout most of their lives. BR did eventually modify the drawgear and No 30800 received No 30755's Urie-designed bogie tender in January 1959.

Opposite top: The extent of the embankment slip can be seen in this picture. The void under the track and the clay bulging all the way to the toe of the embankment are very evident. The quality of these photographs is not of the best, but the locomotive engaged in the recovery operations appears to be an SECR 'E' Class 4-4-0.

Middle: This is a more general view of the pile-up of rolling stock following the derailment. Many wagons were damaged so badly that they had to be scrapped on site.

Bottom: This view looking from the Charing side of the derailment shows the damage to the rolling stock and scattering of the loads. One of the loaded wagon was carrying 6 cwt logs and these required the attention of a crane to reload them into alternative wagons to recover them from the site. Seventeen of the wagons were broken up on site, and removed piecemeal, and four more were loaded up into other wagons to be dismantled elsewhere. Five wagons needed significant repairs to return them to traffic, and thirteen were examined and overhauled and sent forward to their destinations. One of the wagons destroyed was an ex-LNER 'Boplate E' (No E228940), quite a significant casualty.

Left: The void under the sleepers at the point of derailment is shown in this picture where the clay embankment has slipped and the ballast has followed it. The track consisted of 95lb bullhead rail in cast-iron chairs on wooden sleepers, and the ballast was stone, although there was a mixture of clay and ash supporting it. This was fairly typical of Eastern Section permanent way.

Recovery took place but the line was not fully cleared until 19 December. Recovery of the goods posed an especially difficult task. Wagons had to be taken on the down line to the site under the blockage, and the goods, and the remains of the destroyed wagons, loaded into them. A small crane was needed to recover some logs weighing 6cwt.

The inquiry concluded that the clay embankment failed because of an exceptionally dry summer followed by a wet November, which had resulted in cracking of the clay and pockets of water under the track. It was also satisfied that this would not have been visible to the permanent way staff who attended the area until the actual moment of failure. There had been a suggestion from the evidence of damage and destruction caused to the wagons that the train may well have been exceeding the 15mph temporary speed restriction, and this might have contributed to the catastrophic failure of the formation. However, the inquiry panel dismissed this suggestion.

Further slips occurred on this section over the next few years, and a programme of stabilisation of the embankments was started. This included holding the toe of the bank with piling and replacing the top clay with Meldon dust. The total cost was £68,000, which was spread over six years.

The railway's report contained an inventory of the wagons involved, and this is shown in the accompanying table.

Wagons forming the 9.50pm Ashford to Hither Green freight train derailed between Charing and Lenham, 9 December 1949

Wagon	No	Owner	Wagon type	Load	Damage
1	66548	LNER	Van	Bales of paper	One headstock broken, end badly damaged, four axle guards bent, vacuum standpipe broken, box front broken, slipper displaced, derailed all wheels
2	608194	LMR	Mineral	Coal	one headstock grazed', one Gedge coupling broken, two end door boards broken, one end door locking bar broken, three axle guards bent, one brake pin guard and stay iron bent, derailed all wheels
3	72	Fordham	Mineral	Coal	one headstock broken, three axle guards bent, underbearer broken, two brake push rods bent, two end boards broken, two corner plates broken, one buffer face broken, one bearing on nozzle of journal broken, derailed all wheels
4	94526	LMR	Not known, probably high goods	Returned empty boxes	Wagon badly damaged and broken up, derailed all wheels
5	95282	LNER	High open	Empty	Wagon badly damaged and broken up, derailed all wheels
6	47559 (or 47759)	SR	Van	General traffic	Body badly damaged and broken up, underframe loaded up, derailed all wheels
7	228940	LNER	Bogie plate	Empty	Wagon badly damaged and broken up, derailed all wheels
8	1717	Fountain & Burnley	Mineral	Sugar beet	Wagon badly damaged and broken up, derailed all wheels
9	34334	SR	High open	Sugar beet	Wagon badly damaged and broken up, derailed all wheels
10	29605	SR	High open	Empty	Wagon badly damaged and broken up, derailed all wheels
11	414527	LMR	High open	General traffic	Wagon badly damaged and broken up, derailed all wheels
12	7271	SR or MWT	High open	Sugar beet	Wagon badly damaged, loaded up, derailed all wheels
13	595	Airedale	Mineral	Timber logs	Wagon badly damaged and broken up, derailed all wheels
14	4360	Bolsover	Mineral	Not known	Wagon badly damaged and loaded up, derailed all wheels
15	69238 or 62938	LMR	Not known	Not known	Wagon badly damaged and broken up, derailed all wheels
16	13115	SR	High open	Not known	Wagon badly damaged and broken up, derailed all wheels
17	212529	LNER	High open	Not known	Wagon badly damaged and loaded up, derailed all wheels
18	610237	LMR	Mineral	Not known	Wagon badly damaged and broken up, derailed all wheels
19	224757	LMR	High open	Not known	Wagon badly damaged and broken up, derailed all wheels
20	241492	LMR	High open	Not known	Wagon badly damaged and broken up, derailed all wheels
21	301262	LMR	Not known	Not known	Wagon badly damaged and broken up, derailed all wheels
22	Not known	PO	Mineral	Not known	Wagon badly damaged and broken up, derailed all wheels
22	893 or 8939	Stephenson Clarke	Mineral	Not known	Wagon badly damaged and broken up, derailed all wheels
23	723609	LNER	Not known	Not known	Wagon badly damaged and broken up, derailed all wheels
24	3848	PO	Mineral	Empty	Overhauled and forwarded to destination
25	9444	PO	Mineral	Empty	Overhauled and forwarded to destination
26	618827	LMR	Mineral	Empty	Overhauled and forwarded to destination
28	7094	PO	Mineral	Empty	Overhauled and forwarded to destination
29	C1	PO	Mineral	Empty	Overhauled and forwarded to destination
30	3109	PO	Mineral	Empty	Overhauled and forwarded to destination

Wagon	No	Owner	Wagon type	Load	Damage
31	289025 or 289225	LNER	Not known	Empty	Overhauled and forwarded to destination
32	328	PO	Mineral	Coal	Overhauled and forwarded to destination
33	604711	LMR	Mineral	Coal	Overhauled and forwarded to destination
34	3615	PO	Mineral	Coal	Overhauled and forwarded to destination
35	6383	PO	Mineral	Coal	Overhauled and forwarded to destination
36	4604	PO	Mineral	Coal	Overhauled and forwarded to destination
37	P89980	PO	Mineral	Coal	Overhauled and forwarded to destination
38	346281	LMR	Mineral	Coal	Buffer rod broken
39	60221	LMR	Not known	Empty	Headstock broken, underboards broken, buffer spring and buffer guides broken, recker rail adrift (badly damaged)
40	55458	SR	Brake van		Door light and end light broken, tight working doors, buffer cylinder coil broken

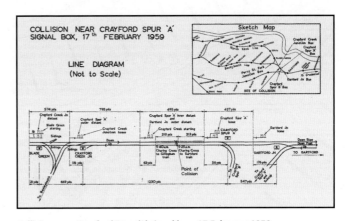

Collision near Crayford Spur 'A' signal box, 17 February 1959.

Crayford Creek Junction and Crayford Spur 'A' Junction

Collision between electric passenger trains, 17 February 1959

The 9.40am Charing Cross to Gillingham service, formed of a 10HAP unit, ran into the rear of the 9.25am Charing Cross to Dartford service formed of a 10EPB (2+4+4) standing at Crayford Spur 'A' home signal. The weather was foggy, but it would appear that the signalman at Crayford Creek Junction signal box had cleared the starting signal irregularly, allowing the second train to enter the section already occupied by the previous train. The speed of collision was estimated to be 15mph.

The impact drove the first train forward 24 feet, and caused the buckeye coupler between the two trains to couple. The force of the collision was absorbed by the eighth and ninth coaches telescoping by 9 feet. Damage was caused to the rear coach of the first train and the leading coach of the second.

There were fifty passengers in the 9.25am train and 150 in the 9.40am. Seventeen passengers were taken to hospital, and all but one were discharged the same day after treatment. One person sustained a broken ankle. Two members of staff in the 9.25am train suffered minor injuries. No damage was caused to the track or signalling.

The signalman at Crayford Creek had omitted to send 'Train Entering Section' for the first train and to observe the block instrument return to the 'Train on Line' position as a consequence. The signalman at Crayford Spur 'A' was therefore unaware that a train was approaching his home signal, and because of the fog he did not observe it arriving. The fog was thick, but the motorman of the first train stated that he was able to see the signal box as he stood at Crayford Spur 'A' home signal.

The action of the first train entering the section automatically replaced the block instrument in Crayford Creek Junction to 'Line Blocked', which, on Sykes two-position instruments, is the same indication as 'Normal', so the Crayford Creek signalman assumed that the first train had gone and that he had missed the 'Train out of Section' bell signal for it. When he tried to obtain a second release for the second train the Sykes instrument correctly refused to release the starting signal, but the signalmen, after consultation, and through poor communication about which train was involved, used the release key procedure to obtain a second release of Crayford Creek's starter, which was then cleared to admit the second train.

Of the trains involved, the rear two coaches of unit No 5021, which was at the rear of the 9.25 Charing Cross to Dartford train, were damaged beyond economic repair. Driving Motor Brake Second No S14061S, and Trailer Second No S15021S were subsequently scrapped. Trailer Second No S14121S was repaired and transferred into new unit No 5302. The withdrawn carriages were replaced with Driving Motor Brake Second No S14062S from unit No 5031, and Trailer Seconds Nos S15023S and S15123S from unit No 5023 involved at Maze Hill were inserted into No 5021.

Following investigation, the Inspecting Officer concluded that the signalmen were jointly responsible for the accident.

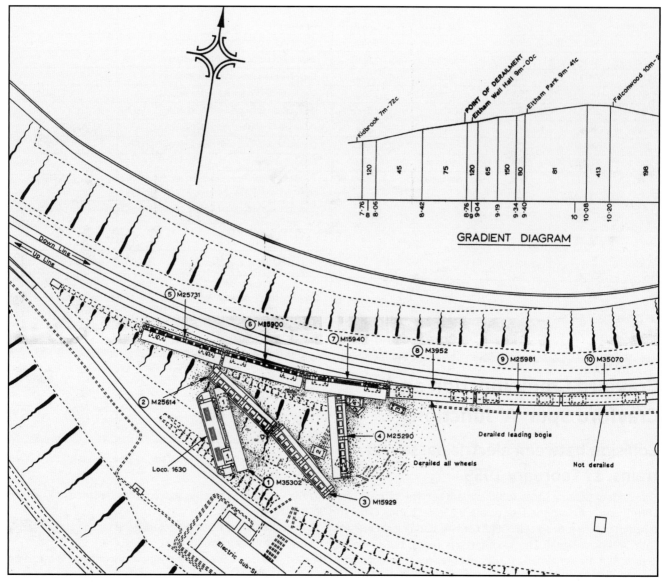

A site plan adapted from the Inspecting Officer's report. *Ministry of Transport, Crown Copyright Reserved 1973*

Eltham Well Hall

Derailment of a passenger train on a curve, 11 June 1972

At 21.36 on Sunday 11 June 1972, on a sharp curve in the up line a few yards on the London side of Eltham (Well Hall) station, a high-speed derailment of a passenger excursion train occurred.

The train was the 20.05 Margate to Kentish Town staff excursion train comprised of ten London Midland Region Mark 1 corridor coaches, well filled with passengers returning from a day's outing at the seaside. The locomotive was LMR 'Brush Type 4' Co-Co diesel-electric No 1630. On a cloudy but dry evening, shortly before dusk and in good visibility and running under clear colour light signals over a route with easily identifiable landmarks, for reasons that will be discussed later the driver failed to take any braking action to reduce his train's

speed on the steeply falling gradient through Eltham Park to Eltham (Well Hall) in preparation for entering the 12-chain-radius right-hand curve just beyond the latter station.

There is a permanent speed restriction of 20mph through this curve. Normally this is not a particularly high risk, compared to somewhere like Morpeth on the North Eastern Region, which has a similar sharp curve at the end of a high-speed section. This is because all passenger trains over this route are starting from a station stop at Eltham Well Hall. These trains are also composed of comparatively lightweight electric multiple unit vehicles that are less prone to turning over at speed compared with a diesel locomotive, which has a much higher centre of gravity.

Locomotive No 1630 entered the curve at about 65mph and overturned to the left, dragging the train after it. The locomotive, after sliding across a coal yard on its nearside, came to rest about 135 yards from the point at which it had started to overturn, and 13 yards from the up line, pointing at

This is the cab of Brush Type 4 No 1630 after the derailment in the former Eltham Well Hall coal yard. Behind it and lying against it is Corridor Brake Second No M35302. The gangway of the second coach, Corridor Second No M25614, is just visible to the left of No M35302. The locomotive has come to rest almost at right angles to the Bexleyheath line. No 1630 was repaired and, following two successive renumberings, was withdrawn as No 47849 in 2002.

an angle towards it; the leading Brake Corridor coach jack-knifed with the locomotive and came to rest alongside and parallel with it, upright but having lost one bogie, which finished lying upside down on the side of the locomotive. The first four coaches careered across the coal yard, where some of their buckeye couplings parted, and the second, third and fourth coaches zigzagged. They finally came to rest in the shape of a letter 'N' when viewed from above. The other six coaches kept generally upright and in line under the constraint of their couplings and, although mostly derailed, they ran on, at a tangent to the track that they had left and past the 'N' of the zigzagged coaches, to come to a stand with the leading end of the fifth coach some 5 yards to the left of the up line and 19 yards past the derailed locomotive and first two coaches.

The fifth, sixth and seventh coaches were all generally in line but leaning over to the left, and the eighth, ninth, and tenth were upright and in line, with the side of the seventh in contact with the end of the zigzagged fourth coach. The tenth coach remained on the rails, as did the rear bogie of the ninth.

Three passengers in the train and the driver lost their lives in the accident, and 126 people, including the secondman on the locomotive, were injured; forty of those taken to hospital were detained, some of them being very seriously injured. Unfortunately two further passengers died of their injuries some period afterwards.

The cause of the accident was excessive speed arising from the driver's failure to control his train. It was determined that he had grossly impaired his ability to drive safely by drinking a

The trailing end of locomotive No 1630 is seen here with a bogie from No M35302 lying on top of it.

This is the start of the 12-chain curve as seen from the end of Eltham Well Hall up platform. The 20mph speed restriction 'cut-out' is visible adjacent to the signal, although it could be more conspicuous. The numerals were supposed to be picked out at one time in white, later changed to yellow, to make them more distinctive. The curve has its origins in the planning of the Bexleyheath line. Originally the Bexleyheath Railway Company intended to make a junction with the Dartford Loop line at Lee. This would have provided a virtually straight route across the terrain. However, a landowner with property on this line of route successfully objected to it, so an alternative route from Eltham to Blackheath on the North Kent Line was chosen instead. This required a sharp curve at Eltham, and a deep cutting and another sharp curve east of Blackheath station close to the entrance to Blackheath Tunnel. To add further to their difficulties, another landowner insisted that the line was encased in a tunnel through his land, and a 'cut and cover' tunnel between the junction and Kidbrooke station had to be provided.

Re-railing and clearing up is under way, with the fourth and seventh coaches visible in this picture. Corridor Second No M25290 is perched at right angles to Corridor Composite No M15940. The breakdown cranes are working from the down Bexleyheath line.

considerable quantity of alcohol both before and after booking on duty, including some shortly before leaving Margate, and some more in his cab during the journey. The 18-year-old secondman confirmed that the driver had been drinking before they met, then had some more beer in the BR Staff Association Club at Margate. In fact, he had probably consumed a full bottle of sherry with his brothers, together with a number of pints of beer, before coming on duty – he was 'pre-loaded', to use a modern idiom. After the accident, post-mortem forensic evidence of the driver's blood/alcohol level together with glass fragments found in the cab suggested that a quantity of alcoholic spirits, possibly as much as a quarter of a bottle, had been consumed by him during the trip from Margate to Eltham Well Hall.

The Inspecting Officer had much to say about the attitude of some staff towards drinking alcohol on duty and the laxity of supervision of train crew, who were able to sign on for duty without anyone of a senior grade in a position to review their fitness. However, despite some brave words on the matter it would still be many years before British Railways adopted a 'zero tolerance' of this behaviour.

Eythorne

Collision between trains and road motor vehicles, 24 January and 14 September 1949

At 6.15pm on 24 January 1949 a ballast train previously working between Eastry and Wingham and propelled by 'O1' Class 0-6-0 No 1373 was struck by an East Kent Motor Services omnibus (JG 9928) on Eythorne level crossing. Originally the train was planned to have been propelled to the site from Shepherdswell and haul away afterwards, but because the traffic had been delayed on the Elham Valley line by sheep, it arrived 1½ hours late. When it arrived from Shorncliffe it was deemed to be unwise to propel a loaded train up the gradient in the prevailing weather, so it was hauled to Canterbury Road instead. After unloading the plan was to 'run by' the locomotive with the wagons to haul back, but again another change of plan occurred because of darkness and it was agreed to propel the train back to Shepherdswell instead.

As the train approached Eythorne crossing at about 3 to 4mph it whistled, and the porter attended the crossing with a red light; this he displayed to two cars that were approaching from Lower Eythorne, which stopped. He then noticed the East Kent omnibus approaching down the hill from the opposite side, by which time the wagons were on the crossing and he was unable to show his red light towards the bus. The guard of the train did see the vehicle, and shone his own red light to the bus driver, but to no avail, and the bus collided with the train's brake van. It then rebounded and struck the following bogie rail wagon, damaging it and causing the step iron to go 'out of gauge'. The guard showed his red light to the engine driver who brought the train to a stand.

The Southern Region inquiry concluded that the operation of the crossing was in accordance with the Rules and speculated that the omnibus driver was travelling too fast for the conditions, which were dark and rainy.

The formation of the train was brake van No 62839 leading, two 'Borails' fitted with Robel cranes, seventeen ADS wagons and brake van No 55542, all propelled by former East Kent Railway locomotive No 1373.

The protection of the crossing became a matter of debate between the railway and Kent County Constabulary, but was unresolved before the next incident occurred on 14 September.

At 8.12am on that day the 7.45am freight train from Shepherdswell to Wingham, having just completed the detachment of a wagon at Eythorne, was proceeding on to the level crossing when it collided with a car being driven by a local school teacher. There was wind and rain at the time and the road at the crossing was partially flooded. The locomotive, 'O1'

Class 0-6-0 No 1381, was running tender-first with a wind sheet fixed between cab and tender. The driver had sounded a short whistle as he moved off and shouted to his fireman to sound the whistle again, but the lad of 16 years of age and with only ten months service was not sure what he should do, and by the time a full understanding had been reached the locomotive was already on the crossing. The driver did not observe the motor car until it was too late to take action to stop the train.

The car was damaged and the driver injured, being taken to a doctor by another passing motorist.

Herne Hill

Collision between a steam passenger train and an electric train, 6 November 1947

At 7.34pm on 6 November 1947 the 4.15pm up express passenger train from Ramsgate to Victoria collided with the 6.58pm electric passenger train from Holborn Viaduct to West Croydon as it was crossing Herne Hill South Junction. The steam train was travelling at 10mph and the electric train at 25mph. The locomotive struck the leading coach just behind the driving compartment, forcing it and the next vehicle, which was a Trailer Third, off the track and against the parapet of the viaduct. The collision caused the front of the first carriage, a Driving Motor Brake Third, to swing round and strike the down-side parapet with the rear foul of the up line. The second coach swung into the parapet wall, partially demolishing it, but remained precariously on the viaduct 20 feet above a builder's yard. There were 100 passengers on the West Croydon train, one of whom was killed and nine were taken to hospital with various injuries; a further fourteen complained of minor injuries or shock. No casualties were reported in the steam train.

Herne Hill South. *Ministry of Transport,* Crown Copyright Reserved

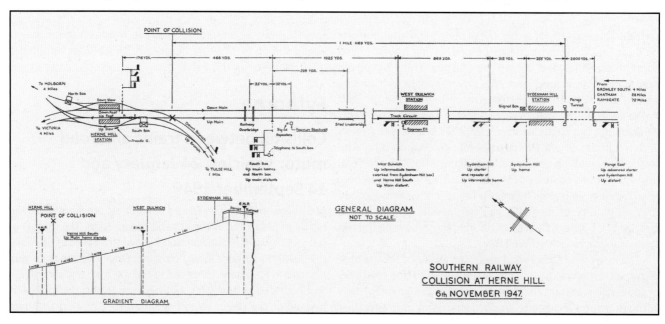

Right: **Seen shortly after the accident and before recovery had started, the precarious position of the front two carriage of the 6.58pm Holborn Viaduct to West Croydon train is graphically illustrated here.**

Below: **Preparing to lift 'U1' Class 2-6-0 No 1901, the breakdown crane has first to clear some of the broken pieces from coach No 9722 of the 6.58 pm West Croydon train out of the way in order to gain access. The carriage was partially over the parapet of the viaduct, so this required great care. This coach was so badly damaged that it had to be broken up on site. No 1901, however, was towed away to Ashford and repaired.**

The extensive damage to coach No 9722 is clearly visible. The non-motorised end of Driving Motor Brake Third No 8678 has been propped up on an accommodation bogie to move it clear while the crane then proceeds to move forward for a tandem lift to re-rail 'U1' No 1901. In the background can be seen the elevated Herne Hill South signal box. The location of the accident on arches high above the South London streets made recovery a delicate and difficult task.

Opposite: Having moved forward, the cranes are now re-railing the locomotive. Tandem lifting was a skilled operation that demanded great expertise by the breakdown gang members. In 1947 there was no such thing as a 'two-way radio' and everything had to be coordinated with hand signals.

'U1' Class 2-6-0 locomotive No 1901 sustained damage to the front end including a fractured left-hand cylinder, and extensive damage to platework. The left-hand connecting rod was also bent. Its train consisted of eight-coach corridor set No 236 and two special cattle wagons, and suffered little or no damage. The formation from the locomotive was BSK 2797, TK 1172, CKs 5586, 5688 and 5682, TK 1170, CK 5683, BTK 2796, and SCVs 3707 and 3728.

The formation of the eight-car electric train was 4SUB unit No 4250 (MBT 8678, TT 9722, TT 9709 and MBT 8844) and 4SUB unit No 4318 (MBT 8163, TT 9453, TT 10367 and MBT 8164).

Damage sustained included:

8678 – solebars and frame badly bent, trailer bogie badly twisted, damage to motor bogie pivot and damage to roof conduits

9722 – bodywork badly damaged, frame and bogies severely twisted, coach broken up on site

9709 – one solebar and headstock bent, one bogie badly damaged, damage to step boards, step irons, coach end and roof, power jumper receptacles broken

8844 – buffer rod bent and power receptacles broken

8163 – two buffer castings broken

The enquiry ascertained that the driver of the 'U1' had failed to stop at Herne Hill South's up main home signal, which was at danger.

The distant signal for Herne Hill South was at West Dulwich, beneath Sydenham Hill's up intermediate stop signal, and was at caution, and a ganger acting as fog signalman was on duty there. He had placed a detonator on the line, which the Ramsgate engine exploded, and was displaying a yellow hand signal light. He believed that the driver and guard had seen his caution but he did not recall hearing the train brakes being applied and it continued to coast by him.

There was thick fog at the time and a relayer was the fog signalman stationed at Herne Hill North's distant signals, being

on the same gantry as Herne Hill South's home signal. As the signals were at caution and danger respectively, he had placed a detonator on the line 40 yards from the signal and displayed a red light to the driver. The detonator had exploded correctly, but the train continued by him at about 20mph. He blew his whistle to try and attract the attention of the engine crew, then displayed his red light to the guard and shouted 'jam your brakes on'. He then telephoned to the signalman.

There was some conflict of evidence between the crew of the 4.15pm from Ramsgate and the fogman. The fireman stated that the fogman at Herne Hill South home signal was displaying a yellow hand signal light, and he informed his driver of such, but the fogman, a man of considerable experience, maintained that he was correctly displaying a red aspect. After extensive questioning, the investigating officer, Lieutenant-Colonel G. R. Wilson, concluded that the fireman, who was comparatively inexperienced, did not fully understand the significance of a detonator at a signal with stop and distant arms on the same post, and had made an error by misinforming his driver. In return, the driver had placed too much reliance on the inexperienced fireman, and had failed to check for himself. It is interesting that the fogman at Herne Hill South's home signal maintained in his evidence that he did not see any of the footplate crew looking out.

The evidence of the guard of the Ramsgate train was also confused, giving one version of events to the internal SR 'Formal Inquiry' and another version to the Ministry of Transport Inquiry. He was not prepared to say that he saw the fogman's red hand signal but maintained that all he saw was a 'red ray' at footboard level about that point and heard a shout. He originally stated that he had made a light brake application, and subsequently excused himself for not making a full brake application as it might have 'parted a coupling'.

The Inspecting Officer was critical of the crew for failing to pay close enough attention to the signals in fog and for the driver in placing too much reliance on his fireman, whose experience in such conditions was negligible. He also considered that the guard could have saved the day, but failed to rise to the occasion and must share a portion of the blame.

Lt-Col Wilson also commented that the use of two detonators at a caution aspect and three at an outer home signal at danger, as was practised on the Great Western Railway, should be considered, instead of having only one at each type of signal as used by the Southern Railway. He also commented on the disadvantage of operating right-hand drive locomotives on routes signalled for left-hand reading.

It would be another twelve years before the semaphore signals were replaced by colour light signals, which were much more reliable in foggy conditions.

It was sadly ironic that just thirteen days earlier there had been a very serious accident at South Croydon, and on the same day another serious accident had occurred at Motspur Park Junction, both of these in similar foggy conditions.

Herne Hill

Collision between the 8.55am boat train from Victoria to Dover Marine and a light engine, 30 June 1957

A further collision occurred at Herne Hill at 9.04am on Sunday morning 30 June 1957 when the 8.55am boat train from Victoria to Dover Marine struck a light engine, Class 'V' 'Schools' No 30920 *Rugby*, which had just started away from

Herne Hill station. *Ministry of Transport, Crown Copyright Reserved*

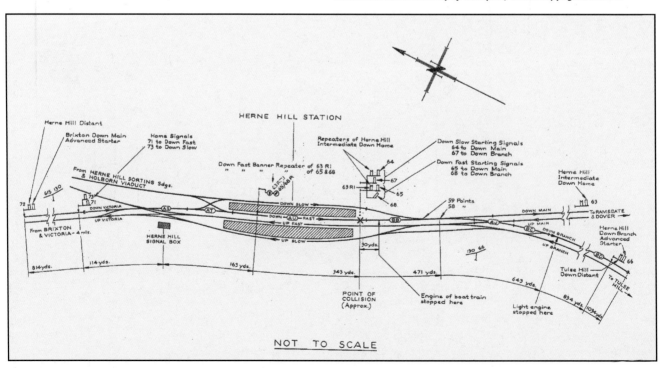

This picture was taken in 1966, nine years after the collision, but shows the exact spot from which No 30920 was starting when it was struck in the rear by No 34088. The signalling has changed considerably since the accident and the array of semaphore arms that can be seen on the plan were replaced in 1959 by this single four-aspect colour light signal with junction indicator above.

the down fast to down branch starting signal en route from Stewarts Lane to Eardley Sidings. The boat train was formed of ten bogie vehicles and a luggage van, and was hauled by 'light Pacific' No 34088 *213 Squadron*. By this time, Herne Hill South signal box had been abolished and in 1956 control of the junction and associated signals had been transferred to a new cabin at Herne Hill North.

The light engine had been brought to a stand at No 68 signal, down fast to down branch, awaiting the passage of a West Croydon service, and was just being signalled to proceed

when the boat train passed No 71, the down Victoria line home signal, at danger.

The passed fireman in charge of No 30920 was alerted by his fireman that there was a passenger train bearing down upon them through the station. The fireman jumped clear on to the station platform, but the passed fireman remained at his post and immediately opened the regulator in the hope he could out-run the errant express and so lessen the impact. He had just managed to proceed but was rapidly overtaken and pushed 300 yards after the inevitable collision. The tender of the light engine was badly damaged, while the passed fireman suffered head injuries and concussion. For his courageous action he was subsequently awarded 10 guineas (£10.50) at a presentation by the Motive Power Superintendent on 23 September 1957.

The driver of the boat train was taking signal aspects verbally from his fireman as they approached Herne Hill. At Brixton he asked his fireman, 'How many off?' to which he received the reply, 'Two,' which he took to mean that the Brixton down main advanced starter and also the Herne Hill distant were clear. He told the enquiry that he had satisfied himself that Herne Hill's home signal was 'off'. He then said he saw the pair of banner repeaters at the station for No 68 starting signal and No 63 distant for Herne Hill Intermediate Block Signal showing 'off' above 'on'. It was not until he was 100 yards from it that he saw the light engine. The boat train was travelling at about 32mph at that time. He made an emergency brake application and warned his fireman that there was going to be a collision.

Both locomotives were damaged, although the 'Schools' Class tender fared worse with a bent main frame and smashed buffer beam. The 'Battle of Britain' Class loco also sustained a smashed buffer beam.. The train was formed of two loose Open Seconds (Nos W3986 and S1308S), Set 452 comprising Corridor Brake Second No S3576S, two Corridor Composites (Nos S5519S and S5534S), two Corridor Seconds (Nos S784S and S797S), a further Corridor Composite (No S5533S) and Corridor Brake Second No S3577S. There was then a further loose Corridor Second (No S1246S) with a four-wheeled PMV at the London end of the train (No S1570S). Of these, Nos S1308S and S3576S were telescoped; the former was fitted with a Pullman gangway, and the latter a British Standard gangway, which were pushed back into the coach superstructure. As well as these two vehicles sustaining significant damage to underframe, bodywork and internal fittings, Nos W3986, S5519S, S5534S, S784S and S3577S also sustained some damage at the ends of the underframe and damage to internal fittings.

The driver of the 'Schools' Class locomotive, a passed fireman, was taken to Kings College Hospital and detained overnight for observation following severe concussion. Passenger casualties were mercifully light: nineteen persons were treated at the scene by London Ambulance for bruises or mild concussion. Two passengers who also sustained shock were taken to Kings College Hospital but were discharged straight after treatment the same day.

It was remarked that when the 'Schools' locomotive came to rest the passed fireman in charge of it, despite his injuries, opened the injectors and tried to throw out the fire.

Both an internal Southern Region Formal Inquiry and a full Ministry of Transport Inquiry chaired by Colonel McMullen were held, and both held that the driver of the boat train was culpable, in that he failed to correctly observe the signals and passed Herne Hill's No 71 home signal at danger. The guard of the boat train was also blamed for not keeping a look-out as the train approached Herne Hill, although in fairness the brake

in which he rode did not have either periscope or side lookouts.

The SR inquiry also found fault with the Herne Hill signalman for failing to notice that he had a Signal Passed at Danger until it was pointed out to him by an S&T lineman who was in the box at the time, and for then not applying the emergency detonator placer to alert the driver of the over-running train. Each was given a disciplinary punishment. As mentioned earlier, the passed fireman was rewarded for his courageous action.

Herne Hill Sorting Sidings

Collision between an electric train and a light locomotive, 1 April 1960

At 6.28am on Friday 1 April 1960 the 6.14am electric passenger train from Holborn Viaduct to West Croydon composed of eight cars collided with a Class 'C' 0-6-0 locomotive standing on the down line at Herne Hill Sorting Sidings. The engine was positioned with the chimney leading, and the leading carriage struck the tender, forcing the engine forwards 160 yards along the line. The motorman was killed, the driver of the steam engine was injured and was detained in hospital, and the passenger train guard and twelve passengers were treated for minor injuries and shock. The front of the motor car of the West Croydon train was wrecked and the underframe badly damaged. Damage to the locomotive was comparatively light, the tender buffers, buffer beam, tender trailing wheels and axle boxes sustaining damage, while the tender tank sprang a leak.

The events leading up to the collision were complex and the Inspecting Officer's account was as follows:

'The engine concerned in the collision was the pilot engine for the Down side at Herne Hill Sorting Sidings. It had been sent that morning to Camberwell to be attached to the rear of the 5.22am Brockley Lane freight train comprising a similar engine and seventeen wagons with a brake van at either end, which had travelled there via Nunhead and Loughborough Junction in the Up direction. It had drawn the train, with the train engine still attached, on the Down line to the Sorting Sidings box and had been uncoupled. The train had then been pulled by its own engine over the crossover from the Down to the Up line controlled by shunt signal No 11 until it was clear of shunt signal No 28, which controls propelling movements from the Up line into the Up sidings.

'Because of prevailing fog, which prevented signals being exchanged between the driver and the guard, the freight train, which was about 160 yards long, had been drawn along the Up line until the engine was opposite the porters' room on Loughborough Junction station platform. There the driver had been told by a porter, who had been advised by the signalman at Sorting Sidings box, that shunt signal No 28 had been cleared

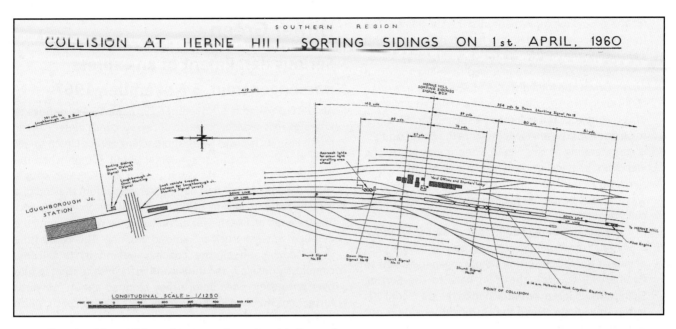

Herne Hill Sorting Sidings. *Ministry of Transport, Crown Copyright Reserved*

Herne Hill Sorting Sidings down home signal No 19, seen here in 1955, was irregularly cleared by the signalman so that the 6.14am Holborn to West Croydon train ran into the tender of 'C' Class 0-6-0, which was standing at shunt signal No 14. At the time of the accident the distant arm seen here had been replaced by a three-aspect colour light signal as the approach lights for Herne Hill signal box, but the function of the signal was materially the same.

for the propelling movement into the Up sidings. The train was being propelled into the Up sidings past this signal when the collision on the Down line took place.

'The pilot engine had followed the departing train on the Down line for a distance of about 80 yards up to shunt signal No 14, where it had been halted while the driver waited for the points to be set and for the signal to be given for the engine to run into the Down sidings; it was standing at this signal when it was hit by the electric train. It will be seen from the sketch that shunt signal No 14 is 76 yards from the signal box; the engine was 13 yards beyond it, judging from the marks of the collision on the ground.

'The working of the freight train as described above is a regular movement except that the Up sidings pilot engine at Herne Hill Sorting Sidings is generally sent to Camberwell to draw the train back to the Sorting Sidings, when it remains attached to the train until it is in the Up sidings. When the Up sidings engine is not available, the Down sidings engine is sent, and it returns to the Down sidings after drawing the train back to the Sorting Sidings signal box, as was intended on this occasion.'

There were slight overtones of the 1915 Quintinshill accident about this one. The Herne Hill Sorting Sidings signalman was unofficially working past his normal booking-off time to assist his relief to arrive for early shift. He also did not use a reminder appliance to tell him that he still had a locomotive standing ahead of his home signal. Despite the fog, neither the driver nor the fireman of the light engine reminded the signalman that they were standing at the shunt signal No 14 either by sounding the whistle or going to the signal box, and the signalman forgot about the locomotive. He then accepted the West Croydon passenger train and cleared his signals. On this occasion he accepted his lapse, but also stated that he had to visit the toilet at the time that he accepted the passenger train, all of which contributed to his forgetfulness.

Hither Green

Serious derailment of an express passenger train, 5 November, 1967

At 21.16 on Sunday 5 November 1967 the 19.43 Hastings to Charing Cross service, made up of two six-coach diesel-electric multiple units (DEMUs) was approaching Hither Green under clear signals on the up main line at about 70mph when the leading pair of wheels of the third coach struck a small wedge-shaped piece of steel that had broken away from the end of a running rail, and became derailed towards the down main line. The train ran on like this for about a quarter of a mile until the derailed wheels struck a diamond crossing. This caused the third coach, and all the coaches behind it, to become completely derailed, and the second to the fifth coaches to turn over onto their sides before they stopped about 250 yards further on. The coupling broke behind the leading coach, which was not derailed, and it ran forward and stopped 220 yards beyond the second coach and some 750 yards short of Hither Green station. The overturned coaches were very severely damaged. The initial derailment occurred 712 yards south of St Mildred's Road bridge between Grove Park and Hither.

The train was well filled, with passengers standing in the corridors of the corridor coaches. Regretfully, forty-nine passengers were killed and seventy-eight injured; of the latter, twenty-seven were seriously injured and were detained in hospital. The majority of the casualties occurred in the overturned coaches.

Both the up and down main lines were blocked and the derailment caused widespread dislocation of the train service.

The weather was cold and damp, and it had rained heavily during the previous week.

The line between Chislehurst and Hither Green is extremely busy, and 419 trains were scheduled to run on it daily from Monday to Friday, 268 on the main lines and 151 on the local lines.

On 4 February 1962 the main lines had been resignalled with multiple aspect colour lights controlled from Hither Green signal box as part of the Phase 2 Kent Coast electrification scheme.

Schematic of the site reduced from the (BR(S) plan.

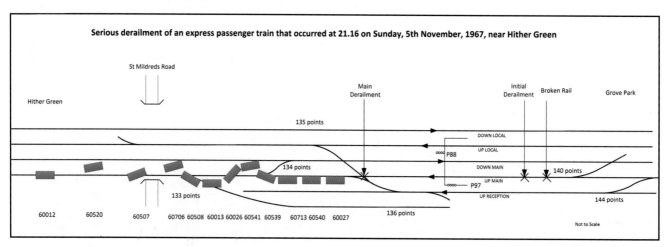

Above: **The scene at Hither Green after the derailment as recovery work takes place.**

This official picture shows the broken rail after removal to a laboratory for forensic investigation. The triangular piece is the part that caused the derailment. *Crown Copyright Reserved*

At the time the maximum permitted speed of DEMUs on this line was 75mph.

The track where the derailment occurred had been laid in February 1967. It was 110lb per yard flat-bottom rail and was the second of two 'closure' rails in the transition between 109lb per yard jointed track and 110lb per yard continuously welded rail. A 5-inch triangular piece of the railhead had come out from the end of the rail due to a fracture running through the last fishbolt hole.

The train was formed from DEMUs Nos 1007 leading and 1017 trailing. Each set comprised, from front to rear, a Motor Second Brake, two Trailer Open Seconds, a Trailer Corridor First, a Trailer Open Second and a Motor Second Brake, and had a through gangway within each unit. Unit No 1007 was a short-underframe type and was 358ft 9in long and weighed unladen 225 tons. Unit No 1017 was a long-underframe type and was 397ft 9in long and weighed 231 tons. The total length of the train was therefore 756ft 6in and its weight was 456 tons.

The Hastings line diesel-electric sets were built in 1957 and 1958 and were of all-steel construction. They were equipped with the electro-pneumatic and Westinghouse brakes and all coaches had buckeye automatic couplings.

The motor coaches were each powered by a 500hp English Electric diesel engine, which with the generator it drove was situated over the outer bogie of the coach. The generator drove two 250hp electric motors, each of which was nose-suspended and drove one axle of the inner bogie. The short-underframe motor coaches weighed 54 tons 12cwt, and the axle loads were 15 tons 10cwt on the outer bogie and 11 tons 16cwt on the inner bogie. The long-underframe motor coaches weighed 1 ton more and the axle loads were consequently 5cwt greater.

Sets Nos 1007 and 1017 had received their last General Overhaul in August and April 1967, after which they had run some 18,000 miles and 41,000 miles respectively.

On account of restricted clearances in tunnels on the Hastings line, the coaches on these diesel electric sets, which were built specifically for use on this line, were restricted to an overall width of 8ft 0½in. In common with other stock that ran on some sections of the Southern Region where clearance difficulties obtained, the side movement at cantrail level had to be restricted to 3 inches, and in order to enforce this restriction the bogies were of a special design; this included, among other things, coned rubber stops to limit the side-to-side movement of the bolster relative to the bogie frame, which come into action when the side movement exceeded three-quarters of an inch either way. Any track irregularity that caused the bogie to move sideways more than that amount relative to the body would therefore cause sharp contact with the coned rubber stops, which exerted a progressively stopping action to the movement. Should the sideways movement exceed 1 inch in the case of the motor bogies and 1½ inches in the case of the trailer bogies, the bolster came into sudden contact with flat hard rubber stops and imparted a certain degree of shock to the vehicle. In particular, a low rail joint would cause the bogie to turn abruptly into the joint and out again, and this would impart a sharp sideways movement

to the coach body, which would increase in proportion to the lowness of the joint and the speed of the train.

It was clear from an examination of the wheels of the vehicles after the derailment that it was the leading wheels of the leading bogie of the third coach that initially became derailed just beyond the point where the rail breakage occurred. The final fracture of the rail, and of the inner fishplate, probably occurred under the train, and it seems that the wedge-shaped piece of rail that had broken away became jammed in the gap and formed a ramp (see the photograph), thus causing the right-hand wheel to become derailed towards the down main line. This piece of rail was badly battered and, in derailing the wheel, it was evidently sprung out of its position into the 'four-foot' between the rails, where it was later found. The remaining wheels of the train jumped the 5-inch gap left in the railhead and in doing so battered the newly broken end of the railhead and shattered the concrete sleeper under it.

Damage to the carriages of unit No 1007 was as follows:

S60012 MBS – not derailed, auto-coupler damaged and minor interior damage

S60520 TS – derailed all wheels and lying on off side, body side and end destroyed, underframe slightly damaged

S60507 TS – derailed all wheels, leaning slightly to off side, underframe badly damaged, solebar twisted, longitudinals bent, gangway end bent, damage to side at lavatory end

S60707 TF – derailed all wheels, lying on off side, underframe badly damaged, solebars bent, longitudinals bent, gangway end bent, side lights broken

S60508 TS – derailed all wheels, lying on near side, body side and end destroyed, roof torn, underframe end broken off

S60013 MBS – derailed all wheels, leaning slightly to near side, two bogies damaged, brake work bent, nearside of cab roof damaged, gangway bent, underframe slightly damaged, stepboards damaged, one side light broken, underslung tanks damaged.

Damage to unit No 1017 was as follows:

S60026 MBS – derailed all wheels, leaning slightly to off side, two bogies damaged, underframe slightly damaged, off side of cab damaged, underslung tanks and boxes damaged, two door lights broken, one side light broken, step irons bent, interior only slightly damaged

S60541 TS – derailed all wheels, leaning to off side, auto-couplers cut off, jumper receptacle broken, step irons bent, bogie step irons bent, spring hangers bent, axle guard rods detached, stepboard missing, gangway bent, interior only slightly damaged

S60539 TS – derailed all wheels, leaning to near side, auto-couplers cut off, gangway and conduit bent, stepboards missing and brackets bent, lavatory light broken, interior only slightly damaged

S60713 TF – derailed all wheels, leaning to near side, bogie headstock bent, brake safety loops bent, jumper receptacle (at compartment end) missing

S60540 TS – derailed all wheels, leaning to near side, bogie headstock bent, brake safety loops bent, brake block keys missing, stepboards broken and irons bent, interior only slightly damaged

S60027 MBS – derailed all wheels, leaning to near side, auto-coupler cut off, step irons bent, seats adrift

The damage to the track and signalling was extensive. Some 970 yards of plain track and 350 yards of track with points and crossings were destroyed, as were the conductor rails, three electric point machines, two shunting signals and three impedance bonds, and power and control cables in the area were damaged.

The BR Joint Inquiry report failed to find a reason for the fracture, which was still awaiting metallurgical analysis, but concluded that, from the evidence presented, there was no reason to attribute any blame to any railway staff. However, the Ministry of Transport inspecting officer seems to have taken a different view. He was critical of the management and application of track maintenance at all levels on the Division, and of the manner in which this piece of track had been laid. It was a transition point between jointed track and continuously welded rail, and it was found that although the rails thereabouts were supported on concrete sleepers, there was a single wooden sleeper under one side of the rail joint where the fracture occurred. This he considered would not have adequately supported the rail, which would have been subjected to excessive stress from passing trains.

The investigation mirrored that which took place into the Sevenoaks derailment of 1927. A riding trial took place using SR DEMUs at Huntingdon on the Eastern Region main line, and was compared to a similar trial on the Southern Region. Colonel McMullen concluded that the riding of the DEMU was better than satisfactory on the Eastern Region but not so good on the Southern, although within acceptable limits for safety. He recommended that continuously welded rail should be provided on all main lines and heavily trafficked commuter lines as a matter of urgency, and that BR should consider that new rolling stock be fitted with fully suspended traction motors.

Horsmonden

Collision between a train and a road motor vehicle at a level crossing, 17 September 1950

At 1.09pm locomotive No 31731, running light from Goudhurst to Paddock Wood after working the 9.00am empty passenger stock train from Margate to Goudhurst, struck an ice cream van owned by Divitto Bros of Deal at Old Hay private level

This is the view that the driver of the light engine would have had of the crossing as he approached it. He had a clear view of the crossing for 750 yards, and although the line was on a falling gradient in a shallow cutting, while travelling at the maximum permitted speed of 30mph it would have given the driver about 17 seconds' warning of an obstruction. The distance that an approaching up train could be seen from a position of safety by anyone operating the gates in order to cross was 200 yards, reducing their decision time to about 13 seconds.

A close-up view of the crossing shows the usual notices provided for users. The crossing deck is apparently in good condition for a user-worked crossing of this type. Both gates would be swung away from the railway and secured, on both sides, before any attempt was made to cross with a vehicle. The safety of users and also that of trains remains firmly in the hands and senses of anyone using the crossing, to look and listen for the approach of a train.

The road user's view of the crossing is not particularly bad, the road surface is smooth and level, and sufficiently wide for the vehicles of the day, although the fences do leave much to be desired. These crossings were generally quiet for most of the year, users being locals who became familiar with their safe operation, regular visitors such as postmen, farm delivery drivers, and suchlike. Problems of user misuse and danger arose when people unfamiliar with the use of such crossings entered the area, hop-pickers and holidaymakers being good examples. The light traffic use suddenly increased a hundredfold during harvest time, and it was not uncommon to station a relief porter at crossings where this happened, as a temporary attendant.

crossing. The van was destroyed, with the body of the vehicle being carried 200 yards before being flung aside, while the roof and one door remained impaled on the locomotive, which stopped 800 yards beyond the level crossing. Both the van occupants were killed.

The gates of the crossing were operated by the user and opened away from the railway.

The ice cream sellers had visited a farm to sell ice cream and cigarettes to hop-pickers.

The internal investigation attributed the accident to want of care by the users. The Ministry of Transport did not investigate the accident, which unfortunately seems to have been one of many arising from similar causes.

Maidstone East station

Collision between a goods train and an electric passenger train, 17 July 1967

At 15.53 on a dry and sunny Monday 17 July 1967 the 15.28 Class 5 goods train from Ashford to Willesden, consisting of twenty-six loaded continental ferry vans and a brake van, and hauled by electric locomotive No E5010, ran past Maidstone East up main outer home signal at danger and collided at about 15mph with the rear of the 15.54 Maidstone East to Victoria electric multiple unit passenger train, consisting of four coaches, which was standing in the up main line platform.

The passenger train was pushed forward some 76 feet, but was not derailed, although the rear coach was extensively damaged. The locomotive and leading three ferry vans of the goods train were damaged, the second ferry van being derailed.

Maidstone East had been resignalled in 1962 and consisted of a miniature lever power frame operating powered points and colour light signals. All running lines within the station limits were fully track-circuited. The section of the line between Hollingbourne and Maidstone East (Bearsted signal box was switched out at the time of the accident) was worked on the Absolute Block system, using Sykes Lock and Block instruments. The signal box was located at the London end of the station on the down side, separated from the main lines by the down platform and the lines leading to the bay platform and goods yard.

There was a central reversible line between the up and down main platform lines, with connections to the up and down main lines at both ends of the station. In the up direction from Ashford to Maidstone East the line rises almost continuously for 10 miles to Lenham station, then falls for about 5½ miles to a point about a mile before Bearsted station. From this point it rises at a gradient of 1 in 101 to a summit just before the station, and thereafter it is on a falling gradient for 2 miles to Maidstone East station. From a point some 700 yards beyond Bearsted station the line falls at a gradient of 1 in 83 for approximately 1,000 yards, followed by a gradient of 1 in 79 for a further 1,780 yards to a point just under a mile from the country end of Maidstone East. There the line continues to fall at gradients between 1 in 81 and 1 in 289 through Wheeler Street and Week Street tunnels, after which there is a short stretch of level track to the station. Through the station the line is on a falling gradient of 1 in 276.

Maidstone East's up main distant signal was located 2,105 yards from the signal box (1,946 yards from the point of collision) and was first sighted at a distance of 300 yards. The up main outer home signal was at the Ashford end of Wheeler Street Tunnel, 784 yards from the box (625 yards from the point of collision), and owing to the curvature of the line at this point was provided with a repeater 944 yards from the box (785 yards from the point of collision). The up main inner home signal was at the London end of the up platform at Maidstone East.

Maidstone East, 17 July 1967.

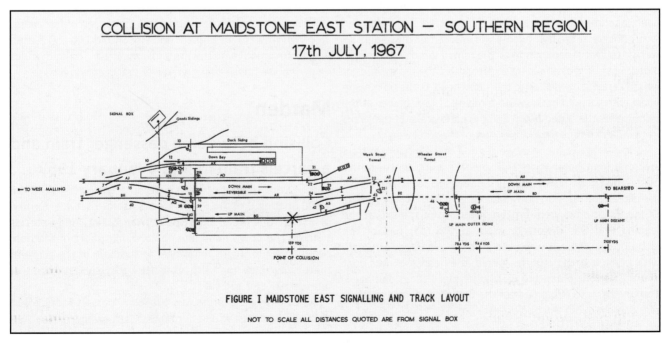

FIGURE I MAIDSTONE EAST SIGNALLING AND TRACK LAYOUT

NOT TO SCALE ALL DISTANCES QUOTED ARE FROM SIGNAL BOX

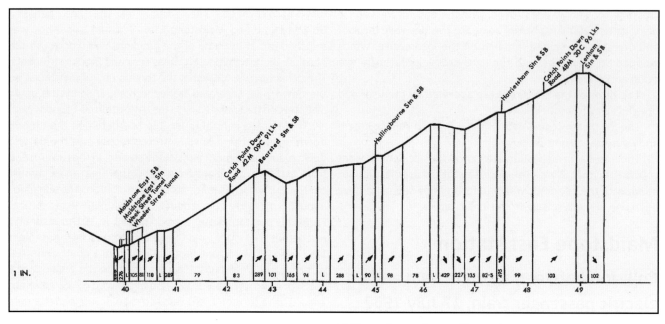

Maidstone East gradient profile, 17 July 1967.

The passenger train consisted of two two-car (2HAP) electric multiple units, built in 1958 and 1963 respectively, of all-steel construction with central buffers between the two coaches of each unit and central buffer plates, and equipped with buckeye auto-couplers at the ends. Side buffers were provided at the outer ends of the units, but were normally retracted, and all buffing force was applied to the centre buffer plates. The units were equipped with electro-pneumatic brakes and air brakes.

The goods train was hauled by British Railways Bo-Bo 750V DC electric locomotive No E5010, of 2,552hp and weighing 77 tons. The train, consisting of twenty-six continental ferry vans, was equal to sixty-seven Basic Wagon Units, and had a 20-ton unfitted brake van, the total weight of the train and the locomotive being 591 tons 10cwt. The vans were all equipped with air brakes and also with vacuum brakes or through pipes. The vacuum brake pipes were connected between the locomotive and the first twenty wagons, but of these only six were fitted with vacuum brakes, the remainder being through-piped. Four of the remaining six ferry vans, the brake pipes of which were not connected to the 'fitted head' of the train, were fitted with vacuum brakes. The combined brake power of the locomotive, the 'fitted head' and the hand brake of the brake van was 138.4 tons, or 23.2 per cent of the total weight.

The damage to the rear two-car unit of the passenger train included bent headstocks and solebars, bent centre buffer plates and auto-couplers, and in the rearmost coach extensive damage to the interior, side and door windows. All the buffers of the locomotive were broken, the front of the cab at the leading end was distorted, while at the rear end of the locomotive, where it was overrun by the leading ferry van, with which it became buffer-locked, the headstock was bent and the various brake and electric jumper fittings damaged. The underframe equipment of the first three ferry vans was also damaged, but the bodies were not.

Damage to the permanent way and the signalling equipment was only slight.

The cause was attributed partly to faulty train preparation at Ashford prior to departure, meaning that insufficient brake force was available to control the train's braking. Although all the first twenty vans were piped up and connected to the locomotive's vacuum brake system, only the first, second, twelfth, eighteenth and twentieth were in fact fitted with the vacuum brake – just five vehicles when at least fourteen were required for a Class 5 goods service.

The driver was also partly at fault because tests demonstrated that the speed of the train between Hollingbourne and Maidstone East was estimated to have been an average of 61mph, 11mph in excess of the permitted speed for this class of train.

The Inspecting Officer queried why the Southern Region was still using the vacuum brake on trains composed of ferry vans, all of which were air-braked, and the SR electric and diesel-electric locomotive fleet were similarly fitted. The authorities agreed to use the air brake wherever practicable in future.

Marden

Collision between a passenger train and a parcels train in fog, 4 January 1969

At 20.42 on 4 January 1969 a collision occurred between the 20.00 Charing Cross to Ramsgate via Ashford service, formed of an 8CEP unit (4CEP units Nos 7117 and 7181), and a parcels train on the down main line about a mile short of Marden, between Ashford and Tonbridge. At the time of the accident there was thick fog with visibility variously estimated at between 25 and 150 yards.

The Ramsgate express was booked to pass Paddock Wood at 20.42. Its driver would normally expect to have a clear run

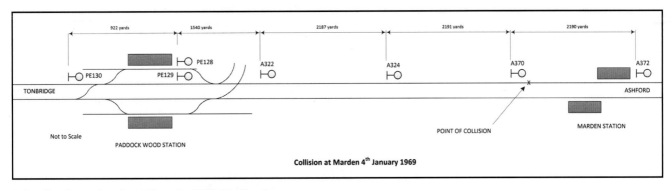

Collision at Marden 4th January 1969

A signalling sketch plan adapted from the BR(S) signalling diagram.

A sketch of vehicle positions.

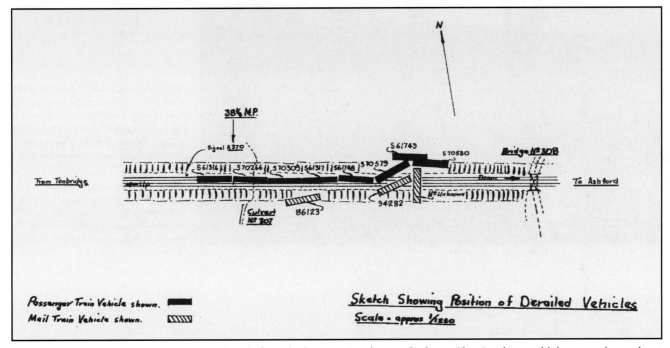

through Marden since the booked train ahead of it, which was the diesel-hauled 19.18 London Bridge to Dover Priory parcels train, was due to pass Paddock Wood 20 minutes ahead of it and to arrive at Ashford, some 21 miles further on, still 18 minutes ahead of it.

On the evening of the accident, however, a track circuit in the down main line through Marden had failed shortly after 19.00, holding A370, an automatic three-aspect colour light signal, at danger. Also, the train immediately ahead of the parcels train, a special rail train that had started from a siding at Paddock Wood destined for Ashford, was some 2 hours late and only 8 minutes ahead of the parcels train; it was also limited to a maximum speed of 25mph. The parcels train, which had been running under clear signals well ahead of the express, subsequently incurred increasingly severe signal checks through Paddock Wood and was stopped at each of the previous two three-aspect signals, A322 and A324, before reaching signal A370. Each cleared from danger to caution automatically as the rail train cleared the sections ahead, the first (A322) clearing just after the parcels train stopped at it, and the second (A324) while the secondman was speaking to the Ashford signalman over the

signal post telephone. The signalman told the secondman about the rail train ahead and the signalling failure, and that he was to telephone again from signal A370, so that although that signal was at caution as he ran up to it, the driver stopped the train while the secondman again spoke to the signalman. This time he was told that the failure had been put right and that the train was to continue its journey in accordance with the aspects displayed by the signals ahead.

Meanwhile the express, which was running some 3 minutes ahead of time at Paddock Wood, was quickly catching the parcels train. As the latter was drawing ahead past signal A370 and had reached a speed of 10-15mph with its rear van a short way past that signal, the express, which had run past signals A322 at caution and A324 at danger, but was still running at some 75-80mph, collided violently with it.

So severe was the impact that the leading coach of the express plunged down the side of the 5-foot-high embankment and came to rest, completely upside down, some 115-120 yards past the point of collision, with its bodywork entirely smashed. The second coach overrode the first and came to rest on its side and very badly damaged, to the right of and

Left: The coaches of 4CEP units Nos 7181 and 7117 are seen here the morning after the collision. At this time there was a livery change taking place and No 7181 was still painted in green whereas No 7117 was in Corporate Blue and Grey livery.

Below: A general view of the recovery that started at Marden on the morning of 5 January. The remote location with no road access over agricultural land made clearing up very difficult.

buckled underframe of the General Utility Van, which was one of last three vehicles of the parcels train, lies upside down on the side of the embankment, its body completely destroyed.

partly ahead of it. The third coach jack-knifed between the second and fourth, one end being dragged down the bank and the other remaining on the ballast. The rear five coaches remained upright and in line, although they were derailed towards the up line but not actually foul of it; damage to them was relatively light and the rear bogie of the last coach remained on the rails. Sadly three passengers and the driver of the train were killed. Eleven other passengers were taken to hospital, and a further number were slightly injured.

After recovery, unit No 7117 was repaired and returned to traffic. Of the coaches of No 7181, Driving Motor Brake Second No S61749 and Trailer Corridor Second No S70530 were destroyed by the force of the collision, and Trailer Corridor Composite No S70579 was so badly damaged that it had to be cut up. Driving Motor Brake Second No S61748 was repaired and eventually placed into 4BEP unit No 7015.

The parcels train comprised eight mixed vans hauled by BRCW/Sulzer Type 3 1550hp diesel-electric engine No 6558. The vans were, in order from the engine, a four-wheeled continental refrigerator van (Interfrigo), two SR-design four-wheeled parcels vans (PMV) built in 1943, a bogie luggage brake van ('Pigeon'), with a steel underframe and a wooden-framed body and panels, a non-gangwayed bogie General Utility Van (GUV), a BR Standard bogie Corridor Brake (BG), a BR Standard GUV, and a BR Standard Covered Carriage Truck (CCT)

The last three vans of the parcels train, although of all-steel construction, were almost completely destroyed. One of them came to rest across the up line, which it blocked, another had one end forced up 15 feet into the air and at right angles over it, and the one ahead was burst open at its trailing end and was buffer-locked with the vehicle ahead, which was damaged. These vans absorbed the shock to the parcels train, the leading vehicles being undamaged and remaining on the rails, though they were propelled forward. The guard was riding in the engine's rear cab and he and the driver and secondman were unhurt. The collision short-circuited both conductor rails, tripping the circuit breakers and cutting off the current. The wreckage of the parcels train, although completely blocking the up line, did not shunt the up-line track circuits.

Rescue and relief arrangements were very severely hampered by the combination of darkness, mud and thick fog, and the remoteness of the site from main roads. Vehicular access was eventually established along narrow lanes and over two recently ploughed fields. The farm manager and staff of Brook Farm came in for praise having provided tractors to transport supplies and personnel from the nearest lane across the fields to the railway.

There was much speculation in the press about the integrity of the signalling system, which was then less than seven years old, and the fact that the signals involved were automatically operated. However, the S&T Department conducted exhaustive tests and was able to demonstrate to the Inspecting Officer that all were working as designed, failing safe, and would not have contributed to the accident. The damage to the driving cab of the electric train was so severe that it was four days before any of the components could be reached. It was then established that the brake had been applied before the collision, but the only conclusion that could be reached was that the driver of the express had disregarded or missed the aspects of A322 at caution and A324 at danger, which might have been difficult to see in the fog, and had not reacted until he had seen the tail light of the parcels train, by which time it was of course too late. A370 would still have been at caution as the express approached because the parcels train, which was 151 yards long, was still in the 200-yard-long overlap and would not have proceeded far enough on to the track circuit section ahead to return the signal to danger.

Maze Hill

Collision between an electric train and a steam train, 4 July 1958

This accident also features in the previous edition of 'SW Special' No 8 'The Other Side of the Southern', but some extra details from the railway's internal report are included here for completeness.

A sketch of the accident site layout from the BR(S) Joint Inquiry report.

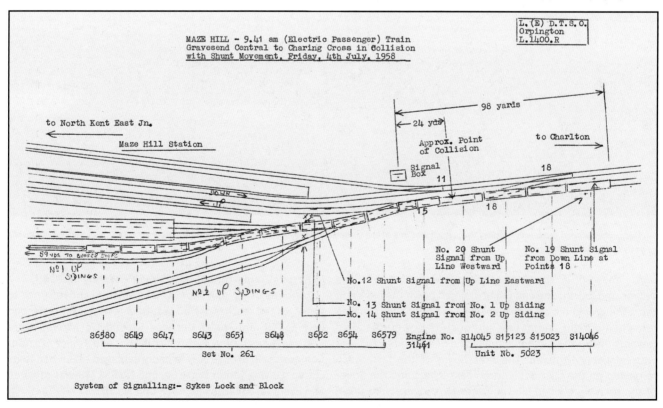

Maze Hill station was the site of a number of carriage sidings where carriages for South Eastern Division excursion traffic were normally kept. On the morning of Friday 4 July 1958 a set of carriages was to be worked from Maze Hill to Herne Hill Sorting Sidings in preparation for working such an excursion. 'C' Class 0-6-0 No 31461 was sent to Maze Hill and at 10.25am was drawing nine-coach set No 261 from No 1 Up Sidings on to the down North Kent via Greenwich line. The set was composed of seven Corridor Seconds (Nos S654S, S652S, S648S, S651S, S643S, S647S and S649S) flanked by two Corridor Brake Composites (Nos S6579S and S6580S). As this manoeuvre was being made the train was run into at about 25mph by the 9.41am electric train from Gravesend Central to Charing Cross formed of 4EPB unit No 5023, with Driving Motor Brake No S14045S leading. The steam locomotive, which was chimney leading, was forced upwards by the collision and was embedded into the cab and guard's van of the electric train, which in turn telescoped with the passenger compartment. The underframe and motor bogie of the electric train and the main frames and headstock of the locomotive were badly damaged. The electric train pushed the steam train back by about 33 yards, and the impact rippled down the train, bending headstocks and truss rods of the steam stock, and the first and second coaches of the electric train. Remarkably the motorman and steam locomotive crew were not killed, but the motorman and guard of the electric train and forty-three passengers were removed to hospital, where five passengers were detained. Despite the cab of the electric train being wrecked, the motorman survived with only minor scratches, and left it by climbing through the window!

The motorman had been on duty since 4.28am and had worked to Cannon Street at 5.48am, working next to Hayes, returning to Charing Cross, then going to Dartford, where he had a break. He then took a train to Gravesend Central before working the 9.41am train from there. It was formed of ten coaches, but six were detached from the rear at Slade Green. The journey from Slade Green to Maze Hill was normal and this was confirmed by the guard.

The motorman admitted that he had observed Maze Hill's up distant at caution, but did not remember seeing the home signal at danger. The train had stopped at Westcombe Park station after passing Maze Hill's distant signal, and on departure Maze Hill's up home signal No 29 was 270 yards beyond Westcombe Park, and had been clearly visible for at least 250 yards after passing under bridge 540 at the London end of the platform. The driver said that he saw the steam train, but assumed it was still in the sidings.

All the signalling equipment was tested and the technicians confirmed that No 30 up distant and No 29 up home signals were 'on', that No 20 ground signal for the shunting move was 'off', and that the interlocking and block controls were working normally.

The Inspecting Officer was unable to find any signalling or other contributory factors to explain this collision and concluded that the motorman should shoulder the blame in this instance. However, as was usual in these incidents, the role of the guard was called into question. He was required by the Rule Book to observe signals and to apply the emergency brake in the event of a driver making an error, and clearly had not done so on this occasion.

Locomotive No 31461 was withdrawn immediately afterwards and sent to Ashford for scrapping. It was cut up in August.

Of unit No 5023, coach No S14045S was also scrapped as beyond economic repair, the unit was disbanded and the remaining carriages used to replace vehicles in other units. Driving Motor Brake Second S14046S was transferred to unit No 5031, which in turn surrendered S14062S to unit No 5021, and Trailer Second Nos S15023S and S15123S were transferred to unit No 5021. The latter unit was subsequently damaged in the Crayford Creek collision on 17 February 1959 (see above).

Mottingham

Collision between an electric train and a light engine, 19 March 1946

At 10.08 pm on 19 March 1946 the 9.40pm down electric train from Charing Cross to Dartford, running under clear signals, collided with the tender of a light engine standing on the down line at the London end of Mottingham station. The London Bridge-based motorman of the electric train was killed and thirteen passengers sustained minor injuries. The Gillingham driver and fireman and the Hither Green guard on the light engine, who were preparing to undertake a shunt in the yard, were shaken by the accident.

The electric train was composed of eight coaches, formed from two three-coach motor units, Nos 1455 and 1265, with two-coach trailer set No 1122 marshalled between. The light engine was former SECR 'C' Class 0-6-0 goods locomotive No 1589, which had arrived at Mottingham to work the 10.25pm goods from there to Hoo Junction.

At the time of the accident the signalmen were changing duty. At 9.50pm an up goods train from Sidcup to Hither Green arrived, running ahead of time, and the locomotive and twenty-five of the wagons drew forward of No 8 crossover in preparation for setting back into the down sidings. The light engine from Hither Green arrived on the down line at 9.54pm and whistled to set back into the sidings through No 11 points ready to form the 10.25pm goods, with wagons off the 9.50pm train. However, the signalman reversed No 8 points and the 9.50pm goods set back into the siding while the light engine remained on the down line, alongside the London end of the down platform.

At 9.58pm Lee Junction offered the 9.40pm Charing Cross to Dartford electric passenger train, but Mottingham refused it, because he was transferring the locomotive of the 9.50pm goods back to the up line to be reattached to the remainder of its train. That done, No 8 points were returned to normal and the down goods train departed at 10.05pm. As soon as No 8 points were normal, the signalman at Mottingham accepted the down passenger train from Lee Junction, having overlooked that there was still another locomotive standing on his down line within the clearing point. He offered the passenger train on to New Eltham and, upon being accepted, cleared all his signals. The passenger train, thus running under clear signals,

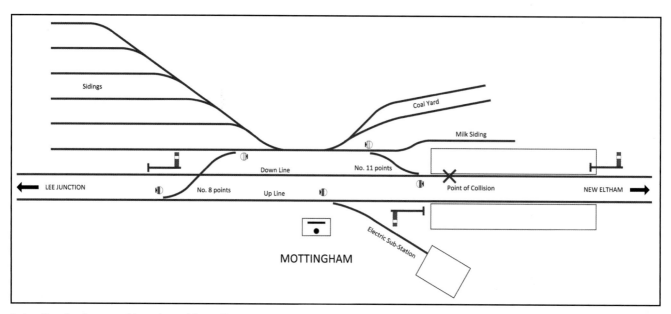

A signalling sketch prepared from the BR (S) signalling plan.

struck the tender of the light engine at about 40mph, driving the whole locomotive forward 53 yards.

The engine's train crew were aware that there was about to be a collision. The guard, seeing the down starting signal come 'off', ran along the platform with a red hand signal, but only managed to reach the bottom of the ramp before the passenger train passed him. The engine driver attempted to release the brake to lessen the effect of the impact, then jumped clear, and both he and the fireman scaled the platform fence and ended up inside a goods wagon standing in the milk siding.

The force of the collision destroyed the cab and leading guard's compartment of the first coach, No 8336, of the leading electric unit, No 1455, killing the motorman, and the underframe at the leading end was severely damaged. The motor bogie was forced back under the coach body by 5ft 3in. This coach was cut up on site. The unit's Trailer Third coach, No 9499, survived virtually intact. The trailing motor coach, No 8335, sustained minor damage to the buffers and coupling.

Coach 8976 of the trailer set No 1122 fared badly, with extensive damage to the headstocks and underframe, and the body stove in at one end. This coach was also broken up on site. However, the other coach, No 9210, suffered no damage. The rear unit, No 1265, suffered much less damage, with only a pair of bolster plates bent under coach No 8098, while the other two vehicles, Nos 9430 and 8097, reported no damage.

Trailer units were the rather poor idea adopted by the Southern Railway from the London & South Western Railway for strengthening trains up to eight carriages at busy times. A motor unit had three carriages, two driving motor coaches with an intermediate unpowered Trailer Car. Off-peak a three-car set was considered sufficient, but at busier times two units could be coupled and, by using multiple unit controls, be driven by one man from the leading unit. The demand for seats (and indeed standing room as well) grew significantly following electrification, so rather than increase the length of the motor sets by inserting another trailer, a series of two-coach trailer sets

While an up Dartford Loop line train runs into the up platform, 'C' Class 0-6-0 No 1257 stands in for its damaged classmate No 1589 for a reconstruction exercise the day after the accident. The locomotive is standing where sister engine would have been when the collision occurred. The tender of this particular locomotive is one of the few that had extended coal sheets, although the locomotive involved in the accident had a tender in original condition. Mottingham station still bears some of the wartime painting practices adopted to help prevent accidents in the blackout. These include the pillars and lamp posts picked out in alternate black and white stripes, and a white-painted edge to the platforms; the latter was adopted universally in 1940 throughout the railway system, and continues to this day. The roof of the damaged passenger train can be seen over the platform fence to the left. The back of No 12 shunt signal can be seen bottom left. Ironically, No 1257, a Hither Green locomotive, was scrapped in 1949, whereas No 1589 was repaired and was among the last Class 'Cs' to remain in traffic.

Looking from the up platform towards Lee, Mottingham's goods yard and signal box can be seen. 'C' Class 0-6-0 No 1257 is now standing in the goods yard prior to shunting on to the down line for a photographic reconstruction of the circumstances of the accident. A down train is approaching, just as the 9.40pm Charing Cross to Dartford train would have done on the previous day. The goods yard looks neat and tidy in 1946, but was to be swept away in the wholesale closure of railway goods yards during the 1960s. Many of the features seen here have since changed. No longer are there lineside cable routes carried on telegraph poles, semaphore signals vanished from this area in the 1970s, the sidings have gone, and much of the lineside is now a linear forest, a haunt of birds and vandals. The siding before the signal box, leading from the up line to the left, was provided to give access to the traction sub-station on the up side, which had no road access.

were created with through multiple unit jumper connections at the outer ends. These were then sandwiched between the motor sets at peak times. At the end of the busy times the trains were broken down into their component parts to operate singly, but this then left the problem of what to do with the unpowered trailer set. At places like Orpington, the eight-coach trains were run into bay platforms at the end of the morning peak, the London-end three-car motor unit detached and the remaining five cars left at the buffer stop end all day, until they joined up in the afternoon for the evening business rush. This meant that during the day passengers detrained away from the exit barrier, and on wet days walked a considerable distance in the rain.

The arrangement was inconvenient and not usually adopted at the London termini to avoid cluttering up platforms with spare stock, so the suburban stations bore the brunt.

These residual five-car sets with blind end leading would frequently be shunted into carriage sidings, to clear the platforms. However, with the driver's cab window obstructed by a pair of carriages, this manoeuvre carried considerable risk. It partially negated the operational advantage of multiple unit stock. With wartime blackout conditions the risks noticeably increased, and by 1940 the Southern Railway was already proposing to abandon the use of trailer sets.

During the period of conversion of the three-coach suburban units to four cars, usually referred to as 'augmentation', trains might be formed from a combination of pairs, three- or four-car units with trailer sets still being used between pairs of three-car units. For a period in the late 1940s this was an operational nightmare, and for passengers the appearance of a seven-car train instead of an eight-car one an uncomfortable nuisance.

The stove-in cab of coach No 8336 from unit No 1455 was put into the coal sidings on the down side at Mottingham awaiting investigation and disposal. Here it is seen standing in the coal yard, and a set of coal merchant's scales stand alongside in the coal bins. This coach was broken up and replaced with No 8391 from unit No 1483, which with the other coaches of unit No 1455 were reformed as 4SUB unit No 4470 by the insertion of six-a-side all-steel trailer No 10340. The set lasted until 1951, when the original bodies were removed and the underframes refurbished and used to make new Bullied-design all-steel six-a-side 4EPB units. The coaches of unit No 1455 had been constructed in 1925 from South Eastern Railway steam stock, the old wooden carriage bodies being placed in pairs on new 62-foot underframes for the electrification of the Southern Railway Eastern Suburban section. The survival of this stock with potentially 50-year-old bodywork came in for much criticism in the 1940s and 1950s. Of the surviving carriages of unit No 1455, No 8335 donated its underframe to No S14001S of unit No 5001, the first of the 4EPB units, while that of No 9499 went to 4SUB trailer No S9019S. No S14001S remained in one of the two very last 4EPB units in service, but despite restoration in early BR livery it failed to secure preservation.

Damage to the tender of 'C' Class No 1589 is pictured here after the locomotive had been taken to Hither Green. The engine was repaired and, as No 31589, survived in BR service until 1961. The 'C' Class were very robust and useful locomotives; 109 were constructed by the South Eastern & Chatham Management Committee between 1900 and 1908, which made them the second most numerous class of locomotives on the Southern Railway, only beaten by Bulleid's 'West Country'/'Battle of Britain' Class 'Pacifics'. Regarded as 'maids of all work', they were used for almost any duty including shunting, goods trains and secondary passenger services throughout Kent and East Sussex, although they could be found as far afield as Southampton and Guildford on occasions, and were no strangers to the North London marshalling yards on transfer freight duties.

Of the trailer unit No 1122, Trailer Third No 8976 fared badly in the collision, and had to be broken up afterwards. This coach had started life as a steam-hauled 48-foot all-3rd Class carriage of SECR origin. It was given air brakes and electric lights in 1925 and was provided with appropriate jumper cables at the outer ends to allow it to attach electrically to the motor units on either side. The jumpers are seen here mounted on a board that concealed the cable connections. The underframe was still the original SECR rod-and-queen-post arrangement, and this fared badly in collisions. The other vehicle of the trailer set was No 9210, a reconstructed and lengthened LSWR carriage on a new 62-foot underframe. This survived to be used firstly to create 4SUB No 4228, formed out of carriages from various ex-LSWR electric units (including Nos 1203 and 1230). In 1955 it donated its underframe to 4EPB carriage No S15385S.

Locomotive No 1589 suffered considerable damage to the tender at the rear with trailing axle boxes and horn cheeks broken, the frames bent, the tank punctured, and all fittings, couplings and buffers at the rear of the tender bent or broken.

The inquiry found that the signalman was at fault for forgetting the light engine. He failed to apply a lever collar to the signal levers even though he had in fact picked one up to do so, but was distracted by a telephone call. The inquiry also found that the crew of the light engine were at fault for failing to carry out Rule 55 by sending the fireman to the signal box to remind the signalman of the presence of the engine on the running line.

Paddock Wood

Derailment of locomotive hauling a local train, 16 March 1949.

At 6:47am on Wednesday 16 March 1949 the 4.50am London Bridge to Margate train became derailed on No 21 catch points at the country end of Paddock Wood down local line. The locomotive concerned was No 30932, a 'V' Class 'Schools' 4-4-0 named *Blundells*, hauling three carriages (Set 635, comprising BT No S3472, CL No S5501 and BTL No S3544) and four vans (Nos W2879W, E175456, S778 and S1534).

As recounted in the text, the 4:50am London Bridge to Margate passenger train hauled by Class 'V' 4-4-0 No 30932 and comprised of three-car 'Rover' set 635 and four vans started against No 9 signal (down local to Maidstone starting) at danger, at the country end of Paddock Wood station, and became derailed on No 21 trap points. The route ahead had been set for a shunt move from the down *through* line to the down Maidstone branch line. This picture, copied from the contemporary *Star* newspaper, shows the locomotive and tender toppled over following the derailment; No 30932 was unique in having a 'self-trimming' tender, seen here, which could be distinguished by the raised side sheets.

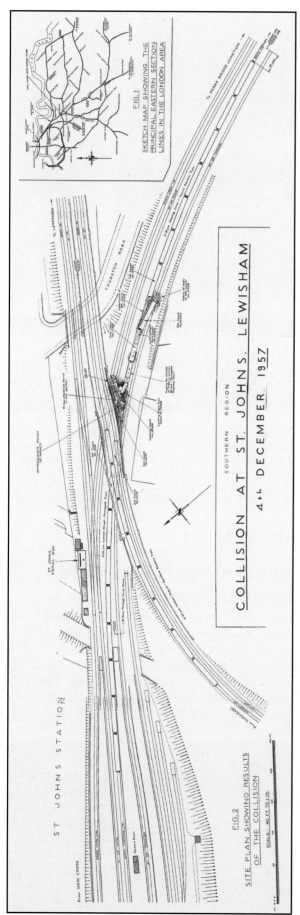

FIG. 1
SKETCH MAP SHOWING THE PRINCIPAL EASTERN SECTION LINES IN THE LONDON AREA

SOUTHERN REGION

COLLISION AT ST. JOHN'S, LEWISHAM

4th DECEMBER, 1957

FIG. 2
SITE PLAN SHOWING RESULTS OF THE COLLISION

SCALE: 40 FT. TO 1 IN.

ST JOHN'S STATION

After the 4.50am train had arrived in the down local platform, before dispatching it the signalman decided to dispose of an empty train standing on the down through line by shunting it via the Maidstone branch line. He therefore operated No 7 signal (down through to Maidstone starting), but was then surprised to see the passenger train starting. He immediately returned No 7 to danger, displayed a red flag from the signal box and attempted to attract the driver's attention by shouting. The driver of the empty train, observing this, sounded his whistle and a lineman standing on the platform also became aware of the mistake and attempted to warn the guard and station staff.

The station foreman, having completed station duties, had hand-signalled to the guard that he was ready to start. The guard had then immediately given the 'right away' signal to the driver. Neither of these members of staff were able to see the starting signal, which was concealed by the station roof.

On inquiry the driver stated that, having received the 'right away' from the guard, he looked at the signal and saw it was 'off', but it must have been No 7 and not No 9 that he observed. The guard, too, after rejoining his van failed to observe No 9 signal, which would have come into view shortly after the train started.

The locomotive thus continued past No 9 signal at danger and became derailed on the trap points, falling to its left side with the tender also derailed. Only one person complained of minor injury but declined treatment.

St John's (Lewisham)

Serious collision between a steam train and an electric train, 4 December 1957

The worst railway accident on the Southern Region occurred in the evening of Wednesday 4 December 1957 just east of St John's station near Lewisham on the South Eastern main line. The trains involved were all running late and out of their booked paths, and all were also heavily loaded. The weather was foggy and it was already dark. The following is a short version of events, while the book by Peter Tatlow, which analyses the circumstances and aftermath in great detail, is recommended (*St John's Lewisham, 50 Years On, Restoring the Traffic*, Oakwood Press).

The 5.18pm Charing Cross to Hayes train, composed of ten coaches, was standing at Parks Bridge M5/M8 signal while the signalman at Parks Bridge attempted to determine the identity of a preceding diesel multiple unit train for Hastings. It seems that he may have missed a train description and therefore had lost track of what was approaching. The 'Walkers' train describer did not distinguish between electric or diesel trains, nor did it store train descriptions in sequence, so required the signalman to observe each description as received. In fact, the 5.25pm Charing Cross to Hastings diesel train was running ahead of the 5.18pm Hayes train and, because of confusion over its identity, had been brought to a stand at Parks Bridge

An extract from the location sketch plan in the accident report.
Ministry of Transport, Crown Copyright Reserved

'Battle of Britain' Class 4-6-2 No 34066, hauling the 4:56pm express from Cannon Street to Ramsgate via Chatham, is seen here on the morning after the collision still embedded in the rear of the 5.18pm Charring Cross to Hayes train, Driving Trailer Second S77565 of 2EPB unit No 5766. Considering the force of the collision the actual damage to this carriage was remarkably light. Unit No 5766 was only a year old, having been released new from Eastleigh in November 1956; even so, the damage was such that it was broken up after the accident.

M10/M12 down through signal for the signalman to find out if it was the 5:18pm train or not. This was necessary because M12 was the junction signal for the turnout from the down through to the Mid Kent line. The Hayes train, 3 minutes behind, was therefore stopped at M5/M8 while this took place.

Meanwhile the 4.56pm Cannon Street to Ramsgate train was itself 76 minutes late approaching St John's, and 9 minutes behind the 5.18pm Hayes service. Unfortunately the original misidentification was taking some time to clear up, and the Hayes train was still at a stand with its rear coach 138 yards ahead of St John's starting signal L18.

Middle: This is the view from the country side of bridge No 111 after the recovery work had started.

Right: The Driving Motor coach of unit No 5766, No S65380, fared badly, with both the front and rear severely damaged. The motor bogie was sheared off and ended up under the underframe of No S14408S, which was the rear motor coach of unit No 5204, leading the 5;18pm Hayes train. The bodywork of No S14408S was totally destroyed by No S65380, which rode over it. Unit 5204 was disbanded after the accident, the surviving motor coach, No S14407S, ending up in unit No 5225, and the trailer cars in unit No 5020.

Neither the driver nor fireman of No 34066 *Spitfire*, the 'Battle of Britain' Class 4-6-2 hauling the 4:56pm Ramsgate train, appear to have properly observed the signals leading to St John's, because their train passed L18 signal at danger, and without any appreciable reduction of speed collided heavily with the rear of the Hayes train at about 30mph. The collision stove in the end of the last carriage of the latter, Driving Trailer Second No S77565 of the rear unit, 2EPB No 5766, and forced the leading carriage of that unit, driving motor coach No S65380, over the underframe of driving motor coach No S14408S at the rear of 4EPB unit No 5204, demolishing the body entirely. Coach No S65380 was sheared off its bogies and the driver's and guard's compartments were demolished. The next vehicle, Trailer Second No S15382S, had the end stove in but otherwise remained intact. Most of the fatalities in the electric train were in No S14408S. The rest of the train remained upright, on the rails and virtually intact.

Bad as this was immediately, worse was to come, because the tender of No 34066 was thrown sideways by the collision and struck the adjacent Lewisham flyover support girders. Thus even before the 4.56pm had stopped moving following the impact, the heavy steel overbridge No 111, which carried the Nunhead to Lewisham lines over the South Eastern main line, was toppled, falling on to the leading three coaches of the Ramsgate train. These vehicles, Corridor Brake Second No S35008 and Corridor Seconds Nos S4377 and S4378, were crushed by the falling girders, the first two completely to the underframes, the third at the leading end. The underframes of these three coaches, all BR Mark 1s, were all less than one year old. More than half of the fatalities occurred in these vehicles.

But now 'Lady Luck' woke up. The 5.22pm Holborn Viaduct to Dartford via Lewisham train was approaching the site of the disaster on the high-level tracks. The motorman observed that the approaching bridge girders were tilted, and immediately applied the brakes. The train halted actually on the bridge, tilted over but not derailed, and the passenger were spared further carnage.

Casualties were heavy. Regrettably eighty-nine passengers died. At least thirty-seven were killed in the 5.18pm Charing Cross train and at least forty-nine in the 4.56pm from Cannon Street. In addition, 109 persons were seriously injured and sixty-seven suffered minor injuries. The guard of the Hayes train also lost his life. Three casualties were difficult to assign to either train, and one further passenger died in hospital.

The enquiry was started by Colonel Wilson and completed by Brigadier Langley, following Col Wilson's death. It was concluded that the driver of the 4.56pm Cannon Street to Ramsgate train was responsible for failing to keep a good look out and observing signals from New Cross to St John's. The Inspector commented on the benefit that the Automatic Warning System might have had in preventing the accident, as well as commenting on the forward vision from the cab of Bulleid 'light Pacifics'. He made the assertion that the 8ft 6in-wide cabs fitted to some of these locomotives to make them compatible for use on the narrow Hastings route (previously described) may have contributed, and recommended that wider cabs be fitted to the members of the class not already so modified. Other matters were considered but were not subject to recommendation.

The fog was, of course, a particular factor, visibility being particularly difficult that night, and many of the signals were in fact situated on the right-hand side of the down through line because of the constraints of the cuttings, bridges and tunnels. This issue was not particularly a problem with diesel and electric traction. Fog signalmen were also not considered necessary where modern colour light signals were installed.

Brigadier Langley also commented upon the provision of more visible tail lights, which he remarked were being investigated by BR. (Red blind experiments were already under way on Hastings DEMUs, although oil tail lamps would continue to be used into the 1960s.) He also commented on the communication between signal boxes, where it was suggested that more up-to-date equipment might have prevented the confusion that led to the Hayes train being stopped, although this could not be considered to be a cause.

Sheerness-on-Sea

Buffer-stop collision, 26 February 1971

At 18.57 on Friday 26 February 1971, the 17.16 ten-coach electric multiple unit passenger train from Victoria to Sheerness, running under clear signals, entered No 1 Platform line but failed to stop short of the sand drag at the end of the line. The leading coach demolished the buffer stops and, without its leading bogie, slid forward across the station concourse, through the booking hall and front wall of the station, coming to rest considerably damaged with the leading cab in the station forecourt. The second coach also partly rose up on to the concourse. The remainder of the train was not derailed and sustained only minor damage.

Sadly, a lady who was standing in the booking hall was killed, and thirteen people were injured, including the driver and guard of the train and the clerk on duty in the ticket office. It was almost dark when the accident occurred, on a clear dry evening.

Sheerness-on-Sea station is situated at the end of a branch line nearly 8 miles long, which joins the main London-Margate-Ramsgate line at a triangular junction just on the London side of Sittingbourne. The branch, which is electrified by the third rail, is double track for the first 3½ miles from the junction with the main line, and thereafter single to Sheerness with a passing loop at Queenborough. The line was worked on the Track Circuit Block System with colour light signals, and was controlled from the signal box at Sittingbourne.

The maximum permitted speed on the branch was 70mph, but there was a 30mph permanent speed restriction from the Dockyard Junction into the terminus on account of sharp reverse curvature and a falling gradient of 1 in 927. The station had two platform lines and a central siding line. No 1 Platform, on the west side, was 854 feet in length and could accommodate trains of up to twelve coaches.

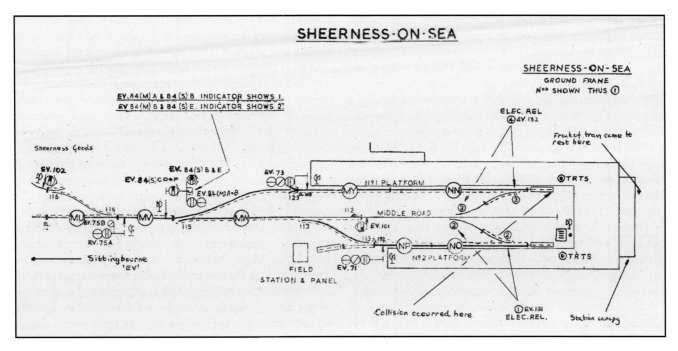

The track and signal layout at Sheerness in 1971.
The profile of the buffer stops at Sheerness.

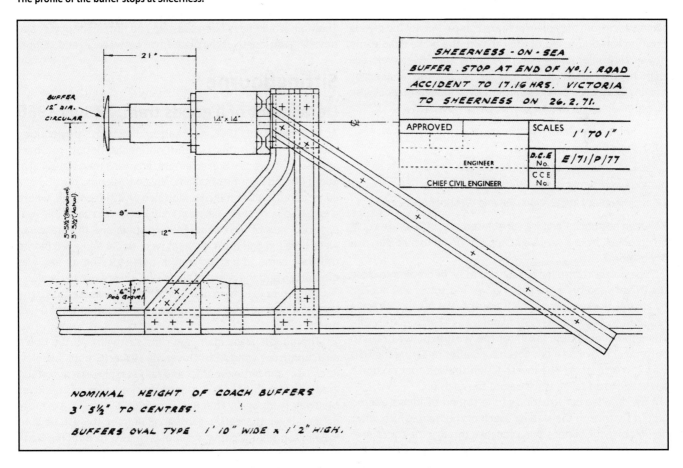

The platform lines were provided with bent-rail-pattern buffer stops preceded by sand drags 20 feet in length, intended to be filled with pea gravel to a depth of 6 inches above rail level for 10 feet, increasing to a depth of 18 inches at the buffer stop. At the time of the accident, however, the average depth of the gravel over the whole length of the sand drag was 6 to 7 inches, and the buffer stops themselves were 2 inches below the standard height of 3ft 5in above rail level.

The station buildings were of timber construction with a roofed concourse extending across the platform ends and, beyond that, the booking hall forming the public entrance to the station with the ticket office adjacent to it directly in line with and beyond the buffer stops of No 1 Platform. The platforms were provided with awnings extending some three coach lengths from the buffer stops, and opening on to No 1 Platform there was a range of staff accommodation.

The ten-coach train was formed of five 2HAP outer-suburban electric multiple units, built for the Kent Coast electrification between 1958 and 1963. Each unit comprised a Motor Second Brake close-coupled to a Driving Trailer Composite. The bodies were of all-steel construction mounted on steel underframes of British Railways standard design and capable of withstanding a buffing load of 200 tons. At the outer ends each unit was fitted with buckeye automatic couplers and vestibule gangway-type centre buffers.

The leading unit was No 6151 with MBS No S61966 leading. The DTC was No S75999, and the following units were Nos 6112 (S61654 and S75076), 6012 (S77126 and S65404), 6149 (S61964 and S 75997), and 6053 (S75371 and S61251). The overall length of the train was 663 feet and its tare weight was 364 tons.

The leading Motor Brake Second was provided with a full-width driving cab without side doors, access being through a sliding door from the adjacent brake compartment. The driving position was on the left of the cab with the brake handle and power controller falling naturally under the driver's left and right hand respectively. The brake handle was applied by moving it forward away from the driver in an anti-clockwise direction, and had five positions:

1. Running position – brakes released
2. Full EP brake application
3. Lap position – Westinghouse brake
4. Service application – Westinghouse brake
5. Emergency application – EP and Westinghouse brakes

Between positions 1 and 2 a variable amount of EP brake could be obtained, from a very slight application up to 50lb per inch at position 2.

The power controller handle had to be depressed to close the Driver's Safety Device (DSD) valve, and power was applied by an anti-clockwise movement towards the driver. The force required to depress the DSD handle was approximately 2lb. The approximate time taken for the Westinghouse brake to become effective on a ten-coach train after releasing the DSD was 2 to 3 seconds. The investigation showed that no brake application had taken place before the collision.

The wooden construction of the station buildings offered little resistance to the leading coach of the train, which, after demolishing the buffer stops, ploughed through the concourse, then carried away a 6-inch-square timber post supporting the main roof girder and destroyed the partition wall between the booking hall and the ticket office, coming to rest with its leading end projecting some 12 feet outside the front wall of the station. The accident also caused a failure of the station electric lighting and cut off the railway telephones.

The body of the leading coach was damaged and distorted, with the driving cab end partially stove in, though the driver's window was only cracked. The leading motor bogie was torn off in the collision with the buffer stops and the trailing bogie of the leading coach then overrode it into the concourse area, all the underfloor equipment being destroyed or badly damaged. The leading bogie of the second vehicle ended up on top of the motor bogie of the first coach, and there was some body damage to the leading end of the second coach. In contrast, there was little damage to the couplings throughout the train, which did not show any signs of heavy impact, the only abnormality being that the centre buffer of the second coach finished up underneath the rubbing plate of the first.

Apart from the destruction of the bent-rail-type buffer stop with its 12-inch-diameter interior-sprung buffers projecting 21 inches from a 14 inch by 14 inch timber beam, and the dispersal of the sand drag, there was no damage to the track, but there was slight damage to the signalling equipment including the release arrangements to the ground frame controlling the crossovers between the centre siding and the platform lines.

From the evidence it would appear that the driver had lost consciousness as the train approached Sheerness. As he did so he slumped over the Driver's Safety Device, holding it down with his body weight and thus preventing a brake application. The train would have been coasting and not under power and travelling the length of the platform at between 10 and 15mph.

Sittingbourne
Derailment of a goods train, 27 July 1966
At 16.47 on 27 July 1966, near Eastern Junction, Sittingbourne, the 14.17 down Hither Green (Continental Depot) to Dover Marine continuously braked empty ferry vans train travelling at about 60mph became derailed on plain track near the end of a curve about a mile on the London side of Sittingbourne, where a long and fairly steep falling gradient begins to ease. The rear eighteen vans of the twenty-four-van train and the brake van were derailed and most of them were badly damaged before the train came to a stand in four portions. The up line was obstructed and the relevant signals on it were put to danger.

There was extensive damage to the track as well as to the vehicles, and normal working was not resumed until 04.30 on the 29th.

The double-track main line runs eastwards in the down direction from London to Dover via Hither Green, Swanley, Rochester and Sittingbourne, and falls steeply (at a maximum gradient of 1 in 93) for 5 miles into the valley of the River Medway, rising again after Rochester, to Gillingham. It is more or less level thereafter through Rainham to just beyond Newington before rising again at 1 in 130 to Bobbing Bank summit. The line then falls at gradients that steepen to 1 in 95 just before Western Junction at Sittingbourne, where the branch northwards to Sheerness diverges, whence it eases to 1 in 210 falling past where the derailment began and to Eastern Junction. It eases through Sittingbourne, then rises again for a short distance on the country side.

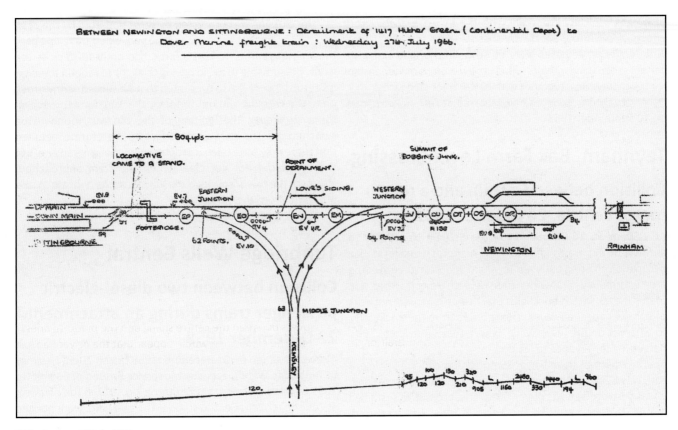

Sittingbourne, 27 July 1966.

In the area of the derailment the line runs in an easy left-handed curve of 1½ miles radius. It had a designed cant of 1½ inches, which gave an equilibrium speed of 55mph. The rails were 95lb bull-head on wood sleepers; they were 18 years old and were programmed for renewal in 1967. The general speed limit on the line was 75mph for multiple unit trains and 85mph for loco-hauled trains, but there was a speed restriction of 30mph from mileposts 32¼ to 34¼, through Rochester, 60mph for nearly a mile through Gillingham, and 65mph over the last mile leading to the summit at Bobbing Bank. Because of previous derailments with this type of vehicle, however, the maximum permitted speed was 45mph, imposed since May of that year.

The train of empty vans and a brake van weighed approximately 388 tons and was drawn by 2,552hp Bo-Bo electric engine No E5002, weighing 77 tons. The train length, including the engine, was 830 feet. The engine was fitted with a compressed air brake, with air connections for working air-braked trains, together with exhauster equipment and a vacuum train pipe for working vacuum-braked trains. With this dual equipment the control system for the air brake was linked by an air-vacuum relay valve to the vacuum pipe so that when the engine was working a vacuum-braked train both the engine and the train brakes were controlled proportionately by the one brake handle. An independent straight air brake with separate brake valves was also provided together with the usual 'dead man's' equipment.

Of the ferry vans, twenty were of 14ft 9in wheelbase, the remaining four of longer wheelbase. They were refrigerator or insulated vans and their equipment included dual braking systems, compressed air and vacuum, and screw couplings. All vans were marked with a letter 'S' in a square surround, which indicated that they were fit to run at 100kph (62½mph) on the Continent. The seventh, which appeared to be the one that derailed first, was Italian State Railways insulated van No 390496. It had a steel riveted underframe with a timber body, and had been built in 1932. The eighth van, No 391410, was of similar manufacture. The brake van was equipped with the vacuum brake only and this system was connected throughout the train, although not operative on the fourth and eighth vans.

The question of the train speed was explored by the Inspector because there had been four similar derailments with this type of train since 1962. The driver gave evidence that at the time of the derailment the train was travelling at 38mph, but calculations comparing signal box and guard's records of passing times indicated that the train must have been averaging 48 to 50mph, and must indeed have been travelling at between 55 and 60mph when the derailment occurred. This would have been in excess of the 45mph permitted speed of the train and vehicles at that point. The rails exhibited wear known as side cutting and, although not at a dangerous level by standards current at the time, may have influenced the derailment. The Joint Inquiry held by the Southern Region therefore determined that the driver was at fault.

The Ministry of Transport Inspecting Officer, Colonel Reed, observed that the same vehicles were operating in Europe at 62½mph without incident, and felt that the track condition may have been a contributory factor. The period from 1960 until the mid-1970s involved a great deal of research into the behaviour of freight vehicles, especially with the as yet undiscovered effects of 'cyclic top'. Short-wheelbase wagons as well as those with longer wheelbases were all suspected of bad riding in certain speed bands. This resulted in new designs of suspension for freight vehicles, together with better track standards.

A very similar accident had occurred at Farningham Road on 10 September 1963.

Teynham, Bax Farm Level Crossing

Collision between a train and a road motor vehicle, 24 October 1952

At 8.50am on 24 October 1952 the 8:20am Herne Bay to Cannon Street train collided with a motor vehicle at Bax occupation crossing between Teynham and Sittingbourne. The area was mainly rural with extensive orchards on either side of the line, as well as brickfields that had an extensive network of narrow-gauge railways carrying bricks from the brickworks to wharves on the River Swale, where they were loaded into barges for conveyance to London.

The train was travelling at 55mph and the motor vehicle, a van, was being driven from the down side on to the crossing; it was destroyed and its driver killed. The locomotive sustained minor damage although the vacuum pipe was fractured, causing the brakes to remain applied. An assisting engine was necessary to clear the line.

Bax Farm Level Crossing, near Teynham.

The crossing was protected by gates operated by the user, and it appears that the driver of the van, when travelling over the crossing earlier to visit a farm, had omitted to close the gates, presumably to avoid having to alight to reopen them on his return trip. It is also presumed that he subsequently drove on to the crossing without properly checking for approaching trains. However, the ignition of the van was found to be switched off. The railway investigators therefore concluded that there may have been a problem with the van's engine, but the driver did not get clear when the train approached, although the driver sounded the whistle at the 'whistle' board 507 yards from the crossing.

The Coroner recorded a verdict of 'Accidental Death'.

Tunbridge Wells Central

Collision between two diesel-electric passenger trains during an attachment, 22 December 1958

At about 1.00pm on 22 December 1958 the 12.20pm Hastings to Tunbridge Wells diesel-electric service formed of 6B unit No 1035 collided with the rear of 6L unit No 1017 in the platform at Tunbridge Wells Central station. The two units were booked to attach to form the 1.03pm service to Charing Cross; however, the 12.20pm service, which had run fast from Hastings, failed to slow down and stop on the final approach and collided heavily with the stationary train. Damage to the cabs of both

The open aspect and visibility at the Bax Farm crossing is clearly demonstrated in this picture. The approaching up train can be seen for a considerable distance. The result of the collision at Tunbridge Wells Central station on 22 December 1958.

units was extensive, and further damage to other vehicles was caused by the shock of the impact. Nineteen persons were injured, including the driver and guard of the 12.20pm train; the driver had to be cut free from his cab. The injured were taken to hospital, and three were detained there, including the driver. There were other minor injuries from flying debris and internal fittings and furnishings being thrown about.

The normal method of operation was to bring the second portion towards the shunter, who stood short of the stationary train displaying a red flag, after which it was conducted slowly forward and attached. The Ministry of Transport did not carry out a formal investigation.

Victoria
Collision between a light locomotive, the 'Golden Arrow' Pullman express, and a passing electric train, 9 December 1949

At 6:42pm on 9 December 1949 a light engine, 'Battle of Britain' Class 4-6-2 No 34085, travelling from Stewarts Lane to London Victoria, overran VE151, the up relief line signal, at danger, and was run into by sister locomotive No 34084. The latter was working the up 4.55pm Dover Marine to Victoria 'Golden Arrow' express, which had been running under clear signals. The collision occurred at No 129 points, up main to up relief

After the collision, 'Battle of Britain' Class Nos 34084 and 34085 were removed to Stewarts Lane locomotive depot for assessment, before being hauled to Brighton for repair. (An earlier less detailed article on this accident appeared in 'SW3', which included photographs of the two engines at Eastleigh, where it had been assumed they were repaired. However, it might have been that only an assessment was undertaken at Eastleigh and the engines subsequently moved to Brighton for repair. In many ways Brighton would be the obvious place, as it had been the main building location for the class.) No 34084 was the train engine of the 'Golden Arrow', and sustained considerable damage from the collision including distortion of the main frames, cracking of the left-hand cylinder casting, much buckling and demolition of platework; the mud-hole plug on the left-hand side of the firebox was also knocked off.

The considerable damage seen here was caused when the left-hand cylinder of No 34084 came into heavy contact with the right-hand cylinder of its sister. At Brighton both locomotives received new cylinders. Neither No 34084, nor its train, were derailed.

crossover, on the approach to Platform 8. As a result of the collision, No 34085 was tipped towards the down local line and struck the side of the 6.40pm Victoria to West Croydon train, which was passing at 30mph. Eight passengers in the latter sustained minor injuries from flying glass.

The 'Golden Arrow' was composed of eight Pullman cars, a baggage box truck and a luggage van. No 34084 sustained a buckled frame and fractured left-hand cylinder casting; the side sheeting of the boiler cladding and the cab were also damaged, and a mud-hole plug was displaced, discharging boiler water and steam. The loss of water caused the firebox plating to

overheat and the fusible plug to melt; this killed the fire, thus preventing further damage, although Fireman Russell, at some risk to himself, was already in the process of throwing out the fire. Minor damage occurred to the baggage truck, and the two leading Pullman cars just above solebar level.

No 34085 sustained damage to the motion, fittings and platework on the right-hand side, the cylinder casting was cracked and the cab side demolished.

The West Croydon eight-coach electric passenger train was composed of unit No 4594 (leading) and unit No 4546. Its last six coaches suffered damage with panels grazed and thirty-one

The cab side panel of No 34084 was torn away in the collision, rendering the locomotive anonymous from this side. The damage to the front corner of the firebox can also be made out, where the removal of the mud plug, used during boiler washouts, was instrumental in rapid and total loss of boiler water, which would have been driven out with considerable force by the 250-280lb boiler pressure. Note that at that time Nos 34084 and 34085 were both in the temporary modified pre-nationalisation livery adopted before British Railways standard liveries were applied. This retained the Malachite green main colour with three horizontal yellow lines. However, 'Gill Sans' lettering and numerals had replaced Bulleid's 'Sunshine' lettering on all new locomotives after about No 34082. No 34084 was nameless at the time and still many months away from receiving its *253 Squadron* identity.

window lights smashed. Most of this damage occurred as the smoke deflector sheet of No 34085 came into contact with the train and was torn away from the smokebox.

Unit No 4546 was formed originally from former LBSCR AC electric stock built for the services to Sutton and Coulsdon. In 1928 these carriages were converted to DC operation with considerable reconstruction so that they conformed to the standard arrangement. These were mounted on 62-foot underframes with a driving cab and motor bogies in the outer cars, and an unpowered trailer between. First Class accommodation was provided in the trailer car and in one of the motor coaches. As reconstructed for DC, the three-car set was numbered 1749, formed of Motor Brake Third No 8716,

Motor Brake Composite No 8884 and Trailer Composite No 9749. Six-a-side 'augmentation' trailer No 10223 was added in June 1948 when the unit number was changed.

As already discussed in the description of the Mottingham collision, during the 1940s the Southern Railway decided to alter the method of using its electric stock to eliminate the difficult practice of handling 'blind-ended' two-coach trailer sets sandwiched between two three-coach motor sets when full-length eight-coach trains were needed at peak times. Originally the individual suburban sets were formed of two driving motor cars with a trailer car intermediately, and off-peak this was considered economic and adequate. It also achieved a reasonable proportion of 1st and 3rd Class

The light engine, No 34085, seen here at Stewarts Lane, sustained damage to platework, motion and fittings all along its right-hand side. The force of the impact cracked the right-hand cylinder casting, and the cab side was demolished. No 34085 was derailed, and placed 'out of gauge' by the derailment, tilting by approximately 35 degrees, and the left-hand smoke deflector was struck by, and caused damage to the windows and bodywork of, the passing 6.40pm Victoria to West Croydon electric train. Both locomotives were comparatively new, and had entered traffic in November of the previous year. No 34085 was eventually rebuilt in 1960, but remained a South Eastern Division locomotive until 1961.

accommodation for off-peak use. However, two motor sets coupled together would increase the proportion of 1st Class without sufficiently increasing 3rd Class accommodation necessary to handle the business traffic, thus from the outset the LSWR added a pair of 3rd Class trailer cars at peak times between the motor sets. The transition between off-peak and peak times required shunting to dispose of the unpowered trailers. The Southern Railway perpetuated this practice in all subsequent pre-war suburban electrification schemes.

Later wartime conditions and restrictions on travel for all but essential purposes obliged the railway authorities in the London area to review the provision of 1st Class, and from 1941 all 1st Class accommodation in Southern Railway suburban trains was declassified within the London Transport region. The issues of having too much 1st Class was thus solved, and it also allowed a rethink of the way that the suburban units were formed and used. Progressively during the 1940s, therefore, spare 3rd Class trailer cars from trailer sets that were already on 62-foot underframes were placed into a three-coach motor set, augmenting it to four cars. The non-standard trailer cars were withdrawn, and replaced with a batch of new stock, with steel-sided bodywork to a wider shape, which allowed six adults to sit side-by-side in the compartment in reasonable comfort, whereas the original pre-war stock could only seat five a side. Increasing the standard suburban train unit to four cars meant that some additional

This is a clearer view of the damage to the smokebox plating and cylinder of No 34085, when it was struck almost side-on by No 34084. Many of the unique Bulleid features visible here, normally concealed under the 'air smoothing', would be swept away in 1960 when No 34085, named *501 Squadron*, was rebuilt to Jarvis's more conventional arrangement.

The damage to the side of the right-hand cab of No 34085 was quite extensive, with all the plating torn away. This occurred as the front of the 'Golden Arrow' locomotive No 34084 that was converging with it, having already scraped along the side of the tender, struck it with full force, also causing No 34085 to tilt over.

Right: **The tender of No 34085 sustained scoring as the 'Golden Arrow' locomotive scraped along its side. This view clearly shows the interim livery applied to the Bulleid 'Pacifics' in early BR days, with the Malachite green and three horizontal yellow stripes, but with 'Gill Sans' 'British Railways' lettering replacing the 'Sunshine' lettering used by the Southern.**

Below: **The 6.40pm Victoria to West Croydon train was formed of two four-coach units, No 4594 leading and No 4546 trailing. This train was passing at the time of the collision, and as No 34085 was tilted into its path it struck and scraped along its side. This caused minor damage to bodywork but broke a number of windows, causing some injuries to passengers. No 4546 is seen here after the accident, and the additional width of the 'augmentation' trailer, added to the three-car set in 1948, is clearly visible.**

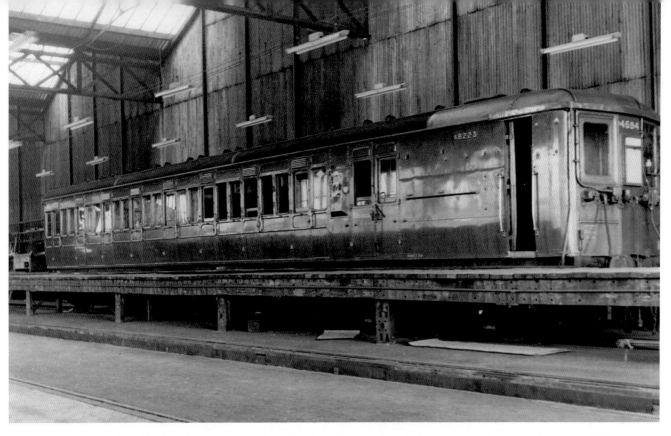

Motor Brake Third No S8223 of leading unit No 4594 is seen here after the accident. Broken windows and minor bodywork damage are visible, in particular the damage to the guard's side lookout.

This close-up of the damage to No S9749 in unit No 4546 gives some details of the bodywork of the former AC coach body. It should also be noted that the underframe differs slightly in detail from those built new for DC stock, as it had previously seen service under AC stock, which in turn was a reconstruction of former LBSCR steam stock. The Southern Railway was noted for its ability to recycle anything that was useful!

Right: **This is a close-up of Motor Brake Third No S8716 in unit No 4546, and shows the damage caused to the protruding guard's lookout, which has been ripped away. Note also the transition from the older LBSCR wooden-panelled finish in traditional style to the steel-sheeted luggage and driving compartment. This was typical of the conversion of steam stock to suburban electric units.**

Below: **This close-up of No S8223 illustrates the different body style, which identifies the origin of the bodywork used to manufacture the pre-war suburban sets. The arrangement of panelling differs noticeably from No S8716, but the steel-sheeted panelling of the luggage and driving compartments are similar. Roof profiles of electric stock also gave a very mixed appearance when coupled into multiple units. In fact, as time went by and carriages were swapped between sets, this variety could be seen even in individual units. The former LBSCR bodies had plain arc roofs but the former South Eastern and LSWR stock had elliptical roofs. The only stock built new for suburban electrification were two batches of units produced by Metropolitan Carriage & Wagon in 1926, twenty-nine for the South Eastern scheme to Orpington and Dartford, and twenty-six for the extension of the former LSWR scheme.**

off-peak mileage was being accumulated, but this was offset by operational simplicity and freeing up space in outer-suburban stations where previously a five-coach set was frequently left at the buffer stops between the peaks.

The inquiry into the Victoria accident determined that the signalling was working correctly and the 'Golden Arrow' was proceeding correctly under clear signals. The driver in charge of No 34085 admitted that he probably misread signal VE149 for VE151, but he could not explain why he did so. That day he had with him an inexperienced fireman, 16½ years old, who had only recently been appointed as a passed cleaner, and not

his usual mate, and it is possible that he did not cross the footplate to verify signal aspects when he should have done. (This accident was also illustrated in 'SW' issues 3 and 5.)

Woolwich Arsenal
Collision between two electric trains, 18 November 1948

At 12:53pm on 18 November 1948 the 12.28pm Charing Cross to Dartford electric train collided with the 12 17pm Cannon Street to Gravesend electric train, which was stationary in Woolwich Arsenal down platform.

The driver of the Dartford train and one passenger in that train were killed, four passengers were taken to hospital, and ten passengers and two members of staff were treated at the scene for minor injuries. The train was composed of unit No 4332 with Motor Brake Third No 8429 leading, Trailer Thirds Nos 9598 and 10348, and Motor Brake Third No 8430.

The Cannon Street to Gravesend train was composed of unit No 4168 with Motor Brake Third No 8792 leading, Trailer Thirds Nos 9413 and 9829, and Motor Brake Third No 8126, which was struck in the rear.

Coaches Nos 8429 and 8126 of the Dartford train were 'telescoped', the underframe of No 8429 being forced under that of No 4168 by 18 feet; the motor bogies under each became detached, and there was extensive damage to both vehicles. The motorman's compartment, guard's brake van and leading passenger compartment of No 8429 were completely wrecked and the second compartment damaged; the motorman's compartment and guard's brake compartment of No 8126 were also badly smashed. The passenger who was killed was travelling in the leading compartment of the Dartford train. The collision forced the standing train, which had its brakes released in preparation for departure, forward by approximately 90 feet. The Inspecting Officer calculated that the speed of impact was approximately 15mph.

The station shortly before Woolwich Arsenal was Woolwich Dockyard, and the platform starting signal there at the country end was Woolwich Arsenal's No 12, a semi-automatic semaphore stop signal. At the time it was working automatically, and when the Dartford train arrived at the Dockyard station it was at danger because the Gravesend train was occupying track circuit 'E' in Woolwich Arsenal station. However, when station

A layout sketch from official report (Ministry of Transport, Crown Copyright reserved)

duties were finished a porter gave a 'right away' signal with the guard who exchanged this with his flag, which the porter then relayed back to the driver as the signal to start. The guard did not observe the aspect displayed by No 12 repeater signal and the driver started the train to proceed. Medway

The next signal, Woolwich Arsenal No 2, was still at 'clear' because the signalman at Woolwich Arsenal had not replaced it to danger after the passing of the Gravesend train, alleging that he had been busy with accepting other trains in both directions. On seeing this, it is possible that the Dartford train driver accelerated, believing the line to be clear into Woolwich Arsenal platform, and because of line curvature and the brick cuttings and overbridges abounding on the route he would not have seen the Gravesend train ahead until it was too late. The Gravesend train had been longer in the station because there was a motorcycle to load into the front brake van.

At that time the onus on observing platform starting signals rested solely upon the driver under Rule 143, and therefore little was made in the inquiry of the actions of the guard and porter in giving the 'ready to start' signal at Woolwich Dockyard, although Colonel Trench did comment upon it, and considered that the guard could have done more by keeping a better look-out. Many, many years later, following further and more serious accidents of this type, which became known as 'Ding, Ding and Away', the British Rail rule book was altered to place onus jointly on the driver, guard and station staff, but this was to be many decades into the future. The failure of the Woolwich Arsenal signalman to replace No 2 signal promptly behind the Gravesend train in contravention of Rule 68 also came in for mention. However, the deceased driver of the Dartford train was ultimately held to be responsible.

On the approach to Woolwich Arsenal, this is the inner repeater for Woolwich Arsenal No 12 semi-automatic intermediate signal under Sand Street Crossing's starting signal. Woolwich Dockyard station is round the corner.

This is the view looking towards Woolwich Dockyard through Dockyard Tunnel.

Accidents to Passengers involving Doors and Windows

The hinged 'slam door' that gave access to individual compartments had been a feature of passenger coaches since railways began. All Southern Region suburban electric stock constructed before 1975, with the exception of the experimental 'PEP' unit, had slam doors. London Transport and the other regions had been fitting their trains with power-operated sliding doors since the 1930s and, in the case of the Underground, considerably earlier, although power operation was still in its infancy up to that time. Surprisingly British Railways did take a step back in the 1950s and reverted to slam doors for replacement stock on the South Tyneside and Watford electric systems and for the Great Eastern electrification.

Unfortunately misuse of doors or defects in the mechanism that secured them meant that here was a potential source of injury, with occasional fatal consequences. Most reported accidents to passengers on moving trains involved the door in some way. Common causes of accidents with doors included passengers opening the door to alight before the train had stopped, a common practice at terminal stations, especially at peak times, latecomers attempting to board trains after they had started, persons seated near the door, particularly children, trapping fingers in the door frame as the door closed, and persons leaning against an insecure door of a moving train. Fortunately the number of serious casualties were not great, amounting to fewer than a dozen each year, but minor injuries ran into thousands.

Above: **Seen here at Slade Green in 1958, 4EPB unit No 5130 has lost two doors and suffered numerous broken windows following contact with a train with a door open on an adjacent line.**

Opposite: **A typical 'slam door' of an electric suburban unit – this one is a 4SUB.**

The interior of a suburban train compartment with the door closed. Note the catch mechanism, designed so that it needed to be opened deliberately and should not be able to open purely by accidental contact. Also note the warning notice above the open window telling people not to lean out. This warning was sometimes corrupted by altering the wording to read 'Do lean out of the window', or other somewhat ruder connotations. In addition, British Railways ran a cartoon-type advert showing a female passenger who had been struck by a door opened before the train had stopped. This appeared both within the trains on partitions walls and also as a poster.

The damage that can be caused to an open door that strikes a train travelling in the opposite direction on an adjacent line. Contact such as this will likely tear the door from its hinges and cause it to strike and break windows and doors on the other train as well. Passengers in adjacent compartments are then at risk of injury from debris and flying glass.

Traditionally doors also incorporated a drop-light window that could be lowered, and despite notices warning against the practice people still put their heads outside the train while it was moving. The South Eastern Division was particularly risky in this respect because historically many of the clearances between the side of the train and lineside structures were not as great as on other parts of the system. Again, numbers of casualties were small, particularly as one would usually need to lean a long way out, but anyone who struck their head against a lineside structure while on a fast-moving train stood a good chance of dying. Such cases often included individuals 'larking about' and voyeurism, when someone was attempting to observe the antics of courting couples in an adjacent compartment.

Attitudes to the slam door have changed over time and what was acceptable in the 1950s is no longer acceptable today. Slam door stock is now outlawed and is now only permitted on heritage lines or where special precautions such as secondary central door locking is incorporated.

The bridges at New Eltham had particularly tight clearances, although reconstruction of No 784 has eased this in part. The author spent many evening peaks supervising this particular station in the early 1970s. A train would arrive from London and many of the doors would be opened to enable passengers to leap off before the train had stopped. This was despite shouted warning by the staff on the platform. The numbers of culprits were overwhelming! On one particular evening the driver got it wrong and overshot the platform by two coach lengths. The leading coaches were therefore under bridge No 782 and, with many of the doors open, there was insufficient clearance to close them. Fortunately they had all been thrown back against the coach side before the train passed the bridge and none had come into contact with the brickwork. The doors of the train that were still at the platform were closed and the train then drew forward slowly until the open doors were clear of the bridge and could be closed from track level. After consultation with the signalman it was decided not to back the train into the platform, so it was 'right away' to Sidcup. A number of passengers in the leading coach were late home for their tea that night as they had to return on the next up train!

A member of staff demonstrates for the coroner's inquest how a passenger who leaned too far out of the window of a moving train came to strike his head on the pier of Bridge 784 at New Eltham.

Fog

The railway suffered from difficult conditions, which occasionally had a tragic outcome as described above, but usually the diligence of the staff prevented an accident. The worst of these conditions included fog, ice and snow, flooding and landslip. The following sections deal with these in turn, beginning with fog.

Quite a few of the accidents on the South Eastern occurred in fog. During the period 1956 to 1970 thick fog was recorded on average each year on twenty-seven days in London and eighteen days at Dungeness. The Thames Estuary was particularly prone to fog, which would drift up the valleys of several tributaries, especially the Ravensbourne, Cray, Darenth and Medway. The worst time was between October and January, with November being a particularly bad month. Before the implementation of the Clean Air Act of 1959, fog around major cities, including London, was a fearsome combination of smoke and fog, referred to colloquially as 'smog'. This combination not only thickened the fog, making the task of the driver doubly difficult, but also had a dreadful effect on the health of the populous. The very worst London 'smogs' were referred to as a 'pea-soupers' reflecting the thick greenish colour of that dish which it resembled, the 'smog' could be tasted too, but the taste was thoroughly unpleasant, being sulphurous and acidic.

Perhaps the most serious effect that fog had on safety was the reduction of the ability of drivers to see signals and therefore to have sufficient warning to react correctly to a danger signal. If visibility was impaired, the driver's sighting

Fog at Dartford on 7 January 1960. Seen from the footbridge, the signal gantry at the London end of the station is barely visible, even as here in daylight; at night with fog the dim oil lamps in the signals would be exceedingly hard to see. Fortunately at Dartford all normal passenger trains would stop in the platform, so would be much closer to the signals prior to starting. However, there were plenty of freight trains passing through Dartford at that time. The signal applications, from left to right, are the Dartford up main starting signal with the Dartford Junction to Dartford Loop distant underneath it; Dartford Junction to North Kent distant; Dartford Platform 2 up starting signal; and Dartford Platform 3 up starting signal. The station here has been extensively remodelled since this photograph was taken.

time on the approach to a signal was reduced and he might not therefore be able to stop at a signal displaying danger. The consequent overrun might bring the train into collision with another standing ahead of the signal.

The distant signal was key to this. This signal was located three-quarters of a mile or thereabouts on the approach to a stop signal, and was distinguished from all other signals by a yellow arm with a black chevron and fishtail cut-out. Unlike all other stop signals it would display a yellow light for 'caution' and a green light for 'all clear' at night. It was a general principle that only if all the stop signals controlled from a particular signal box were clear would the signalman be able to clear his distant signal. It was therefore understood by a driver that if he saw a distant signal displaying a yellow light or having its yellow fishtailed arm horizontal he must expect to be stopped at a subsequent stop signal, and reduce his train's speed in anticipation of this.

The railways developed various measures over the years to counter the difficulties caused by fog. During foggy weather a fog signalmen would be stationed at semaphore distant signals. These men would have with them flags, lamps and fog signals. The latter consisted of a small explosive charge in a metal case, which was attached to the top of the rail with lead straps, and would detonate should a wheel pass over it, making a loud bang. All the while that the semaphore distant signal was at 'caution' the fog signalman had to place and maintain a fog signal on the rail and display a yellow hand signal. If the driver heard an explosion he should look out for a fog signalman holding a yellow flag or light to indicate that the distant signal was at 'caution', and react accordingly.

This system was crude and still relied on the driver knowing where he was and where the stop signal was located after he had encountered a distant signal at 'caution'. No additional warning was provided at stop signals. However, the theory was that if he applied his brake correctly he should stop before reaching it.

The fog signalman had to judge the correct action from the actual working of the signal. If the fog was particularly bad he might have to listen to the movement of the arm and wires, or in more severe cases to actually climb the signal and feel the position of the arm. Some signals were provided with little repeating arms at the base, but these were rare. When the signal cleared he removed the fog signal from the rail. However, the system was not entirely fail-safe.

At busy locations a lever frame was provided, connected by rodding to a placer machine that placed a special type of fog signal on the rail. Instead of lead clips, these signals were carried in a metal holder that was held in the placer arm. Sometimes they were fed into the mechanism from a magazine, but at other locations the fog signalman needed to replace them manually if they were exploded. These detonator placer machines enabled fog signalmen to look after more than one distant signal where multiple tracks were involved. Mechanical fog signal placers were also essential for the safety of the man acting as the fog signalmen in multiple-track locations where clearances were limited.

Various attempts were made over the years to provide the driver with signal indications automatically in the driving cab. An early trial of Kempe and Rowell's patent system took place in the 1880s at Wimbledon. This consisted of a bar in the track that could be raised when a stop signal was at danger, raising a shoe on the locomotive that operated a valve to sound a whistle and apply the brake. The North Eastern Railway under Sir Vincent Raven had trialled a comprehensive system of mechanical ramps that connected to a device in the locomotive cab and gave the driver an indication if a signal was showing an adverse aspect, sounding a whistle and partially applying the brake. However, there were different systems

Left: **A fog signalman's hut adjacent to Sand Street Crossing starting signal. This is a typical Southern Railway concrete example, which offered a modest amount of shelter for the man stationed there. He would also have a brazier made of iron straps into which he would place anything combustible to get a good blaze going to keep himself warm. He is close enough to the signal to see it, but at night or in very thick fog he might need to actually climb the signal ladder to confirm whether the signal was at clear or caution. Just visible in front of the hut is a lever to operate a detonator-placer machine.**

Opposite top: **Fog at St John's on 3 December 1947. Looking in the up direction from adjacent to the flyover (Bridge 111), St John's station is barely visible in the fog. The signal box on the right controlled colour light signals here and at Lewisham. This picture was take ten years to the day before the terrible collision described earlier.**

Opposite bottom: **Another photograph taken on the same day is looking from the end of the local line platforms towards Lewisham – on a clear day it would be possible to see as far as Lewisham station. On the Nunhead line flyover a freight train can just be made out descending towards Hither Green. The signal to the right is L18, which was passed at danger by the 4.56pm Cannon Street to Ramsgate train ten years later.**

This fog signalman's hut at Walworth Road is made of wood, with a lever frame to operate detonator placers on multiple lines. The box in front of the levers with the cable attached contains electrically operated indicators repeating the position of semaphore distant signals. The rodding from one of the levers runs between the tracks from the foreground to a fog signal placer machine in the distance. Another rod run disappears under the track to the left. Note the conductor rail protection boarding to help prevent contact with the 'juice' when the fog signalman went to replenish the machines. (Other images of this type of equipment will be seen in *Southern Infrastructure 1922-1934: Photographs from the E. Wallis collection*, published by Noodle Books.)

under development on the Great Eastern and Great Central as well, and the LNER did not in the end adopt any of them during its existence.

The Great Western Railway did develop a successful warning system before the Great War that consisted of a ramp in the track and a shoe under the engine. As the locomotive passed over the ramp the shoe would be lifted by it and a valve would open and the brake vacuum would start to leak away, eventually applying the brake. However, if the ramp was energised with electricity the valve would immediately close again. Only if the signal was clear was the ramp energised, so an element of fail-safe was built in. The leaking vacuum sounded a horn, and the electricity rang a bell. These different sounds alerted the driver to the status of the signal, and allowed him to take over control, and close the valve himself, and operate the brakes normally. Of course, if he failed to react correctly to the horn, the loss of vacuum would apply the brakes. This system was called Automatic Train Control (ATC). All GWR main lines were equipped with ATC from about 1918.

In 1931 the Stowager-Hudd ATC system was installed experimentally on the Southern Railway at Byfleet. This system used magnetic induction to operate a vacuum valve under the locomotive instead of physical contact between a ramp and a shoe. The inductors would be located at distant signals. However, and in line with the policy also adopted by the London Midland & Scottish and London & North Eastern railways, the Southern placed more reliance on replacing semaphore signals with high-intensity colour lights, and the Stowager-Hudd system was not adopted. The LMS did eventually install Stowager-Hudd equipment on the London, Tilbury & Southend line, but it was not until AWS appeared in British Railways days that a comprehensive warning system was applied progressively throughout Britain.

The Automatic Warning System (AWS) was an amalgamation of the GWR ATC and the Stowager-Hudd system, combining the in-cab functionality of the GWR's system with magnetic inductors rather than mechanical ramps and shoes. By the time it was ready to be introduced, the 'Big Four' had been nationalised and were now British Railways. Priority for the new system was given to main lines where semaphore signals were still commonplace. On the Southern Region it was the Western Division main line that was first provided with AWS, as it had long stretches of automatic semaphore signalling operated on the LSWR pneumatic system. The Central and South Eastern divisions were not given priority, partly because there had been much re-signalling with high-powered colour light signals, which in theory at least were able to penetrate fog and therefore did not need fog signalmen. This was only partially true, and accidents such as the collision at St John's in 1957 might well have been avoided if AWS had been installed.

Other fog precautions that were adopted by the Southern included the use of hurricane lamps placed at the top of the ramp at either end of station platforms to help the driver to locate them. Some selective thinning out of the service was also adopted since, with drivers having to exercise greater vigilance, trains travelled less quickly and therefore journey times were extended.

Fog still had a negative influence on operations despite fog signalmen and latterly AWS. Drivers travelled much more cautiously, looking out for signals and obstructions, and would approach stations more cautiously so as not to overrun, while signalmen might wait until a train driver whistled before clearing a home signal if the fog had obscured the arriving train. This all added to slower working and delay, which with the intensive service in the London suburban area would increase delays cumulatively. The Southern Railway particularly had a policy for dealing with this. Every year a pamphlet was drawn up and issued, which included arrangements for dealing with ice and snow as well, but fog working was also well and truly covered. Examples of the South Eastern Division fog working notices for 1952 and 1957 are included here.

The 1952 pamphlet was a thick book with 72 pages, so only the preamble is included; the rest of it was taken up with a rewritten suburban timetable that was to apply throughout any day when Fog Working was in force.

The policy changed in 1957 when only the peak hours were amended. During off-peak periods normal train services were deemed to run.

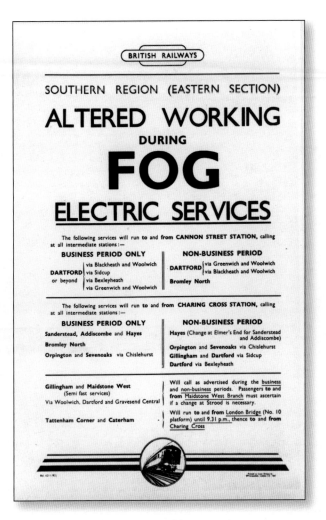

(PRIVATE and not for publication)

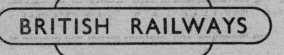

SOUTHERN OPERATING AREA

LONDON EAST DISTRICT

WORKING OF TRAINS

DURING FOG,

ALSO

RUNNING OF DE-ICING TRAINS

OCTOBER 1952, & until further notice

This Notice to be retained until superseded by revised edition.   The information contained in this notice will not be repeated in the Monthly Supplements.

TABLE OF CONTENTS

Waterloo

S. W. SMART,
Superintendent of Operation.

Supp. No.23—1

WORKING OF TRAINS UNDER CONDITIONS OF FOG.

1. **In the event of Fog** being prevalent, and of such density as to warrant the number of trains being reduced, a special service of electric trains will operate as shown herein.

   The Steam Train Schedules and Stations served will operate as shown in the Working Time Tables except as altered herein.

PUBLIC NOTICES TO BE POSTED IN ADVANCE GIVING DETAILS OF THE SPECIAL SERVICE.

   Holders of Season Tickets between Suburban Stations and London may be allowed to proceed by the first available service irrespective of the London Termini served.

2. **The Station Master or Person in charge** of the undermentioned Station or Signal Boxes to advise Control Office, Orpington, when any appearance of fog prevails at any time, and thereafter must report conditions at suitable intervals to **Orpington Control** stating approximate visibility in yards, also whether fogmen are at their posts or have been sent for.

   The term " Fog " must be understood to apply when fixed signals cannot be seen at two-hundred yards.

Charing Cross	Blackheath "A"	Elmers End Box	Swanley Box
Cannon Street	Welling Box	Victoria	Sole Street Box
New Cross	Sidcup Box	Blackfriars Box	Gillingham Inspr.
Hither Green Siding "C"	Dartford Inspr.	Herne Hill North	Tonbridge West Box
Sevenoaks "A"	Gravesend Box	Shortlands Box	Ashford Inspr.
Woolwich Arsenal Box	Catford Bridge Box	Orpington "A"	Faversham Inspr.

   During the months of October to March, inclusive, a weather report **MUST ALWAYS** be telephoned to **ORPINGTON CONTROL** from the above mentioned points, between 4.0 a.m. and 4.30 a.m. **IRRESPECTIVE** of the state of the weather.

METHOD OF INTRODUCING FOG WORKING.

3. To notify all concerned the system of advice to be used, will be that shown below and all such messages will be prefaced with the words "message for transmission to all stations," and be followed by, " Fog service will operate from.........a.m. or.........p.m.

   A record to be kept of the messages received, and also the time they are transmitted.

CONTROL TO ADVISE.	ADVICE TO BE SENT TO
Superintendent of Operation (Control)	——
Electrical Engineer, London Bridge	——
London (East) Divisional Superintendent ...	——
London (Central) Divisional Superintendent...	——
Central Telephone Bureau, Waterloo	——
Motive Power Control, Orpington	Shed Masters, Bricklayers Arms and Stewarts Lane.
Guards' Control, Orpington	——
Lewisham Sub-Station	——
Charing Cross	Waterloo.
Cannon Street	——
London Bridge	New Cross, St. John's, Lewisham and Rotherhithe Road.
Blackheath...	All stations to Slades Green via North Kent and Bexleyheath Lines.
Hither Green	" " Orpington and Dartford, via Loop Line.
Victoria	" " Shortlands (via Main Line) and Nunhead.
Holborn Viaduct	" " Loughborough and Stewarts Lane.

— 3 —

METHOD OF INTRODUCING FOG WORKING—*continued.*

The following Stations shown in column 1 to advise those shown in column 2.

COLUMN 1.	COLUMN 2.
Charlton	All Stations to Deptford.
Lewisham	„ „ Addiscombe and Sanderstead.
Elmer's End	„ „ Hayes.
Dartford	„ „ Chatham.
Hoo Junction (Cabin)	„ „ Allhallows and Grain.
Strood	„ „ Maidstone West.
Maidstone West	„ „ Paddock Wood.
Grove Park	„ „ Bromley North.
Orpington	„ „ Tonbridge.
Tonbridge	„ „ Ashford, Hawkhurst Branch and Hastings.
Robertsbridge	„ „ Rolvenden.
Headcorn	„ „ Tenterden.
Ashford	„ „ Dover Marine, Minster, Ore, Dungeness and New Romney.
Dover Marine	„ „ Sandwich and Selling.
Chatham	„ „ Faversham.
Faversham	„ „ Ramsgate.
Dunton Green	„ „ Westerham.
Shortlands	„ „ Swanley.
Swanley	„ „ Sole Street and Gravesend West.
Sevenoaks	„ „ Eynsford.
Otford	„ „ Maidstone East.
Maidstone East	„ „ Hothfield.
Nunhead	„ „ Crystal Palace (High Level) and Ravensbourne.
Sittingbourne	„ „ Sheerness-on-Sea.
Sandling Junction	Hythe.
Crowhurst	Bexhill West Branch.

At stations where there is a Foreman Motorman or a Motive Power Representative advice to be given accordingly.

4. OPENING AND CLOSING OF SIGNAL BOXES.

To improve the timekeeping during the period when the Fog Working is in operation, Station Masters to specially watch the running of trains and arrange in conjunction with the Control Office to open or keep open, as necessary, Signal boxes under their control which are normally switched out for certain periods.

FINISHING SERVICES.

5. Berthing Stations to notify Control Office at midnight their position so that arrangements may be made in conjunction with the Electrical Department to ensure sufficient Trains terminating at the correct Berthing Stations for the following morning service.

6. **Advice to Motormen, Drivers and Guards.**—Upon advice being received that the Fog Service is being brought into force, or the normal service resumed, the Station Master or person in charge at Junctions and other Stations concerned must satisfy himself that Motormen, Drivers and Guards of Trains are advised, so that they may be prepared for additional stops or otherwise as laid down in this Notice.

In the case of Express Trains, the Staff at intermediate Stations where the Train is booked to call, must acquaint the Driver and Guard if the notification of the introduction of Fog Service is received after the booked departure of the Train from the starting point.

Guards who become spare at Charing Cross or Cannon Street, by reason of the curtailment of services or dislocation of working, must report themselves promptly to the Guards' Representative or Supervisor in charge.

Guards working to Slades Green and Dartford who become spare to report at once (by telephone from Slades Green) to the Station Master at Dartford.

— 4 —

FINISHING SERVICES—*continued*.

Guards working to other stations must report themselves promptly to Guards' Regulating Office by telephone to Orpington Extn. 30, to obtain instructions as to subsequent working.

Depots at which Guards are provided for stand-by trains to keep the Guards' Regulating Office (telephone Orpington 30) advised of arrangements made in utilising these Guards.

Motormen who become spare by reason of curtailment of services, or dislocation of working must report themselves promptly by telephone to the nearest Foreman Motorman.

7. **Telephonic Advice to be sent to Superintendent of Operation, Waterloo (Extension 2130)** not later than 12.0 noon from all Depots and Stations responsible for berthing Steam Trains, giving following particulars of :—

    (1) Surplus Trains or Stock.

    (2) Trains or Stock required.

Stations starting Steam Trains must advise Passenger Rolling Stock Department, Waterloo, and Junction and Terminal Stations in all cases where Trains are not formed in accordance with the booked Carriage Workings.

8. **Availability of Workmen's Return Half Tickets.**—During the time the Fog Service is in force, and the Orpington, Bromley North, Hayes and Addiscombe Line Services are diverted to Charing Cross, Return Half Workmen's Tickets from Cannon Street issued from the undermentioned Stations may be accepted at Charing Cross :—Reference A3/Pad-1/B.

Orpington.	Bingham Road.	Elmer's End.	Hayes.	Lower Sydenham.
Bromley North.	Addiscombe.	Eden Park.	Clock House.	Catford Bridge.
Sundridge Park.	Woodside.	West Wickham.	New Beckenham.	Lady Well.
Grove Park.				

RESTORATION OF NORMAL ELECTRIC SERVICES.

9. Immediately the Fog clears, the Station Master or person in charge of Stations enumerated below will be held responsible for seeing that Control Office, Orpington, is immediately advised by telephoning the Code Word "Fog Clear," so that prompt arrangements may be made to restore the normal Electric service.

STATIONS.	TO ADVISE.	STATIONS.	TO ADVISE.	STATIONS.	TO ADVISE
Charing Cross ...		Westerham ...			
Cannon Street ...		Sevenoaks			
New Cross		Dunton Green ...	Orpington.		
St. John's		Knockholt		Victoria	
Lewisham		Chelsfield		Factory Jc. ...	
Blackheath ...		Bat and Ball ...		Holborn	
Maze Hill		Otford	Swanley.	Loughborough Jc.	
Charlton		Shoreham		Nunhead	
Plumstead		Eynsford		Crystal Palace ...	
Dartford		Greenhithe ...		Bellingham ...	Herne Hill
Park's Bridge Jc.	Control Office, Orpington	Northfleet		Sydenham Hill ...	
Hither Green ...		Gravesend Central		Penge (East) ...	
Grove Park ...		Mottingham ...		Beckenham Jc. ...	
Chislehurst ...		Bexley		Shortlands Jc. ...	
Orpington		Eltham (Well Hall)	Dartford.	Bromley South ...	
Catford Bridge ...		Welling		Bickley	
New Beckenham		Barnehurst ...			
Elmer's End ...		Abbey Wood ...			
Addiscombe ...		Erith			
Herne Hill		Slades Green ...			
Swanley					
Gillingham					
Maidstone East ...					

The Control Office, Orpington, will then advise Starting Stations the time the Normal service will be resumed, and upon receipt of an advice "Normal Service"* the Starting Stations concerned will make the necessary arrangements and advise the intermediate stations concerned. Should it be found impossible to restore any particular service, Control Office to be immediately advised.   *Time to be inserted.*

— 5 —

RESTORATION OF NORMAL STEAM SERVICES.

10. The method of restoring normal Steam Train Working will be as shown above. The Code " Steam Normal " with the addition of the time, to be used.

FREIGHT TRAIN ARRANGEMENTS—WEEK-DAYS.

11. **Freight Trains to and from L.M.R. and L.N.E.R., via Widened Lines.**—During Fog, Freight Trains from Hither Green Sidings and Bricklayers' Arms must not leave Depots after 5.0 a.m. unless authorised by Control Office.

12. **Prohibited Hours for Freight Trains to Bricklayers' Arms.**—During Fog the prohibited hours for Freight Trains from Hither Green Sidings, Mottingham, Blackheath or Catford Bridge to Bricklayers' Arms will be from 5.30 a.m.

   Freight Trains to Bricklayers' Arms will be despatched from Hither Green Sidings, Mottingham, Blackheath and Catford Bridge after 10.30 a.m., under the following conditions :—

   Control Office, Orpington, to regulate the despatch of Freight Trains and only allow them forward by arrangement with the Depot Master at Rotherhithe Road.

13. **Train Engines of Freight Trains impounded** may be worked forward from Hither Green Sidings and other outlying Depots to Bricklayers' Arms between 5.30 a.m. and 10.30 a.m. as opportunity arises, the Control Office, Orpington, and the Depot Masters co-operating, so that the Engines may be worked through with as little delay to Passenger Traffic as possible.

14. **Freight Trains from Hoo Junction to Dartford or Stations above.**—Freight Trains must not leave Hoo Junction between 4.0 a.m. and 9.30 a.m.

15. **Foreign Companies' Mid-day Transfer Trips.**—The Mid-day Transfer Trips from the Foreign Lines must be cancelled and Additional Trips run, if necessary, after 8.0 p.m.

WORKING OF TRAINS UNDER CONDITIONS OF FOG—WEEK-DAYS.

LONDON AREA VIA NEW CROSS AND GREENWICH, ALSO TATTENHAM CORNER AND CATERHAM LINES.

16. **SUBURBAN ELECTRIC TRAINS** will call at all Stations.

   MAIN LINE ELECTRIC TRAINS to Gillingham and Maidstone West will call as booked unless otherwise shown.

   CHARING CROSS TO TATTENHAM CORNER AND CATERHAM Trains will terminate and start from London Bridge Low Level (No. 10 platform), except the following which will run as booked.

Down.	Up.
4.58 a.m. Cannon Street.	8.43 p.m. Tattenham Corner.
9.44 p.m. Charing Cross.	9. 3 p.m. Tattenham Corner.
10. 4 p.m. Charing Cross.	9.23 p.m. Tattenham Corner.
10.24 p.m. Charing Cross.	9.43 p.m. Tattenham Corner.
10.44 p.m. Charing Cross.	10. 3 p.m. Tattenham Corner.
11. 4 p.m. Charing Cross.	10.23 p.m. Tattenham Corner.
11.40 p.m. Charing Cross.	10.43 p.m. Tattenham Corner.

— 6 —

WORKING OF TRAINS UNDER CONDITIONS OF FOG—WEEK-DAYS—*continued*.
LINE AND PLATFORM ALLOCATION—DOWN TRAINS.

17. The allocation of Platforms and Lines will be as follows :—

From	To	Route via	Platform at London Bridge.	Line to North Kent East.	Line at New Cross.	Line from Park's Bridge.
Cannon Street ...	Dartford	Blackheath and Woolwich	1 or 2	1	L	—
Cannon Street ...	Dartford, &c. ...	Greenwich	1 or 2	1	—	—
Cannon Street ...	Dartford, &c. ...	Bexleyheath ...	1 or 2	1	L	—
Cannon Street ...	Dartford, &c. ...	Loop	1 or 2	2	T	L
Charing Cross... ...	Tattenham Crnr.	——	3	—	T	T
Charing Cross... ...	Bromley North ...	——	3	3	T	T
Charing Cross... ...	Addiscombe, Sanderstead and Hayes.	Lewisham	1 or 2	2*	L	—
Charing Cross... ...	Sevenoaks	——	3	3	T	L
Charing Cross... ...	Dartford, &c. ...	Loop (via Lewisham)	1 or 2	2	L	L
Charing Cross... ...	Gillingham ...	Greenwich	1 or 2	1	—	—
Steam Trains from Charing Cross or Cannon St.	... ...	Greenwich	1 or 2	1	—	L
		Dartford Loop ...	1 or 2	3	T	T
		Chislehurst ...	3	3	T	T
		Chislehurst Loop	3	3	T	T

*—No. 1 from Southwark Park when necessary to clear Steam Empties.

LINE AND PLATFORM ALLOCATION—UP TRAINS.

18. The allocation of Lines will be as follows :—

From	Route via	To	Line from Hither Green.	Line from Park's Bridge.	Line from North Kent E.	Line from Southwark Pk.
Dartford or beyond ...	Woolwich and Blackheath	Cannon Street	—	—	3	2
Dartford or beyond ...	Loop	Cannon Street	—	T	1	1
Dartford or beyond ...	Bexleyheath	Cannon Street	—	—	2‡	2
Dartford or beyond ...	Greenwich	Cannon Street	—	—	3	3
Dartford or beyond ...	Loop via Lewisham ...	Charing Cross	L	L	3	2
Sevenoaks	——	Charing Cross	L	T	1	1
Bromley North	——	Charing Cross	T	T	1	1
Addiscombe ... ... Sanderstead ... ... Hayes	Lewisham	Charing Cross	—	—	2‡	1
Steam Trains ...	Greenwich	Charing Cross or Cannon St.	—	—	3	3
	Chislehurst		T	T	1	1
	Dartford Loop ...		L	T	1	1

‡—No. 3 when necessary to clear Steam Empties.

19. **Cannon Street and Charing Cross Local Steam Passenger Working**—These workings, except 9.13 a.m Cannon Street to Charing Cross, will be **cancelled**.

LONDON AREA (VIA HERNE HILL AND CATFORD LOOP), ALSO CRYSTAL PALACE (HIGH LEVEL) AND WEST CROYDON LINES.

20. **SUBURBAN ELECTRIC TRAINS** will call at all Stations.

21. **MAIN LINE ELECTRIC TRAINS** to Gillingham and Maidstone East will call as booked unless otherwise shown.

22. **STEAM SERVICES.**
    All Steam Trains to Charing Cross and Cannon Street will call at London Bridge.

B.R. 31029

(PRIVATE and not for publication)

BRITISH RAILWAYS
SOUTHERN OPERATING AREA
(LONDON EAST DISTRICT)

WORKING OF TRAINS
DURING FOG, ICE AND SNOW

ALSO

RUNNING OF DE-ICING TRAINS

WINTER 1957/1958 and until further notice

This Notice to be retained until superseded by revised edition.

For Electric stock working see separate Notice.

In previous years, when " Fog Service " has operated, a special service of trains has run throughout the day in place of the normal advertised train service.

This arrangement is now discontinued and when, in future, " Fog Service " is introduced, which will be mainly confined to the business periods, the normal advertised train service will continue to run with the cancellations and alterations shown in this Notice.

TABLE OF CONTENTS

Waterloo.

S. A. FITCH,
Chief Operating Superintendent.

Lond. East Fog Supp.—1

3

WORKING OF TRAINS UNDER CONDITIONS OF FOG.

The Station Master or Person in charge of the undermentioned Stations or Signal Boxes to advise ORPINGTON CONTROL when fog occurs at any time, and thereafter must report conditions at suitable intervals stating approximate visibility in yards, also whether fogmen are at their posts or have been sent for.

The term " Fog" must be understood to apply when fixed signals cannot be seen at 200 yards.

Charing Cross.	Blackheath " A."	Elmers End.	Swanley.
Cannon Street.	Welling.	Victoria.	Sole Street.
New Cross.	Sidcup.	Blackfriars.	Gillingham (Inspector).
Hither Green Sidings " C."	Dartford (Inspector).	Herne Hill " A."	Tonbridge " A."
Sevenoaks " A."	Gravesend Central.	Shortlands.	Ashford (Inspector).
Woolwich Arsenal.	Catford Bridge.	Orpington " A."	Faversham (Inspector).

During the months of October to March, inclusive, a weather report **MUST ALWAYS** be telephoned to **ORPINGTON CONTROL** from the above mentioned points, between 4.0 a.m. and 4.30 a.m. **IRRESPECTIVE** of the state of the weather.

1.—PUBLIC NOTICES.

The usual poster " Fog Service in Force " to be exhibited. Holders of Season Tickets between Suburban Stations and London may be allowed to proceed by the first available service, irrespective of the London Terminal served.

2.—OPENING AND CLOSING OF SIGNAL BOXES.

A list of extended signal box opening times to operate when fog is prevalent is included in the " Hours of Opening of Signal Boxes," publication dated 17th September, 1956. In addition, Station Masters to watch specially the running of trains and arrange any further extensions which may be necessary in conjunction with the **Orpington Control.**

3.—ADVICE TO MOTORMEN, DRIVERS AND GUARDS.

Upon advice being received that the Fog Service is being brought into force, or the normal service resumed, the Station Master or person in charge at Junctions and other Stations concerned must satisfy himself that Motormen, Drivers and Guards are advised, so that they may be prepared for additional stops or otherwise as laid down in this Notice.

At Stations where there is a Foreman Motorman or a Motive Power representative, advice to be given accordingly.

4.—METHOD OF INTRODUCING FOG WORKING.

To notify all concerned the system of advice to be used will be that shown below, and all such messages will be prefaced with the words " Message for transmission to all Stations," and be followed by, " Fog Service, will operate from ....a.m./p.m.

The Control will advise points shown in Column 1 who are at once to advise appropriate Stations in Column 2.

In addition each Signalman at a Station Signal Box receiving the message must at once advise the person in charge of the platform.

Stations Masters to satisfy themselves that advice to be given to all staff under their control immediately on receipt of a Fog Message, or as soon as such staff are on duty.

The time at which these messages are received and transmitted must be recorded.

Signalmen switching into circuit after a Fog message has been disseminated are to be given the information.

Column 1	Column 2
Electrical Control, London Bridge	—
H.Q. Control	—
Redhill Control	—
Central Telephone Bureau, Waterloo	—
Guards' Control, Orpington	—
Motive Power Depots	—
Lewisham Sub-Station	—
Charing Cross	Waterloo.
Cannon Street	—
London Bridge	New Cross, St. Johns, Lewisham and Rotherhithe Road.
Blackheath	All Stations to Slade Green via North Kent and Bexleyheath Lines.
Hither Green	„ „ Orpington and Dartford, via Loop Line.
Victoria...	„ „ Shortlands (via Main Line) and to Nunhead.
Holborn Vdt.	„ „ Loughborough Jn. and Stewarts Lane.

4

METHOD OF INTRODUCING FOG WORKING—*continued.*

The following Stations shown in Column 3 to advise those shown in column 4.

Column 3	Column 4
Charlton	All Stations to Deptford.
Lewisham	,, ,, Addiscombe.
Elmers End	,, ,, Hayes.
Woodside	,, ,, Sanderstead.
Dartford	,, ,, Chatham.
Hoo Jn. (Box)	,, ,, Allhallows-on-Sea and Grain.
Strood	,, ,, Maidstone West.
Maidstone West	,, ,, Paddock Wood.
Grove Park	,, ,, Bromley North.
Orpington	,, ,, Tonbridge.
Tonbridge	,, ,, Ashford, Hawkhurst Branch and Hastings.
Ashford...	,, ,, Dover Marine, Minster, Ore and New Romney.
Dover Marine	,, ,, Sandwich and Selling.
Chatham	,, ,, Faversham.
Faversham	,, ,, Ramsgate.
Dunton Green	,, ,, Westerham.
Shortlands	,, ,, Swanley.
Swanley	,, ,, Sole Street.
Sevenoaks	,, ,, Eynsford.
Otford	,, ,, Maidstone East.
Maidstone East	,, ,, Hothfield.
Nunhead	,, ,, Ravensbourne.
Sittingbourne	,, ,, Sheerness-on-Sea.
Crowhurst	Bexhill West Branch.

5.—METHOD OF RESTORING NORMAL SERVICE.

Immediately the Fog clears, the Station Master or person in charge of the Stations shown in paragraph 1 will be held responsible for seeing that **Orpington Control** is advised immediately by telephone.

The Controller on duty will decide when the full normal Service is to be resumed. An advice " Message for transmission to all stations ; Fog service withdrawn from ......a.m./p.m.,'' will be sent through the same channels as shown in paragraph 5.

The time at which these messages are received and transmitted must be recorded.

When the Fog Service continues throughout the day, **normal working will be resumed the next morning unless Fog Service is again advised to operate.**

Fog Service announcement posters should not be left exhibited after the close of the day's service.

6.—GUARDS AND MOTORMEN'S DUTIES.

Guards who become spare at Charing Cross or Cannon Street, by reason of the curtailment of services or dislocation of working, must report themselves promptly to the Guards Representative or Supervisor in charge.

Guards working to Slade Green and Dartford who become spare to report at once (by telephone from Slade Green) to the Station Master at Dartford.

Guards working to other Stations must report themselves promptly by telephone to Guards Controller, Orpington, for instructions as to their subsequent working.

Depots at which Guards are provided for stand-by trains to keep the Guards Controller, Orpington, advised of arrangements made in utilising these Guards.

Motormen who become spare by reason of curtailment of services, or dislocation of working must report themselves promptly by telephone to the nearest Foreman Motorman for instructions as to their subsequent working.

5

FOG SERVICE

MONDAYS TO FRIDAYS.

7. ADDITIONAL SHUTTLE SERVICES.

Addiscombe–Sanderstead and Elmers End.
Bromley North and Grove Park.

From Addiscombe to Elmers End.	From Elmers End to Addiscombe.
5.57 a.m.	6.44 a.m.
6.48 a.m.	7.40 a.m.
7.39 a.m.	7.48 a.m.
8. 1 a.m.	8.19 a.m.
9.14 a.m.	9.25 a.m.
4.42 p.m.	

From Elmers End to Sanderstead.
6. 5 a.m.
6.59 a.m.
5.28 p.m.
6.42 p.m.

From Sanderstead to Elmers End
6.25 a.m.
7.23 a.m.
5.47 p.m.

From Bromley North to Grove Park.
6.26 a.m.

From Grove Park to Bromley North.
6.39 a.m.

8. CHARING CROSS, TATTENHAM CORNER AND CATERHAM SERVICES.

Down trains will start from and Up trains terminate at London Bridge throughout the day up to and including 8.21½ p.m. from Tattenham Corner and 9.31 p.m. from London Bridge. Up trains normally running to Charing Cross and terminating at London Bridge will arrive London Bridge 2 minutes later than booked. 4.58 a.m. Cannon Street to Tattenham Corner and Caterham also 10.43 p.m. Tattenham Corner to Cannon Street will run as booked.

9. THE FOLLOWING PASSENGER TRAINS WILL NOT RUN.

From Cannon Street.
6.19 a.m. to Sanderstead.
6.45 a.m. to Hayes.
7. 5 a.m. to Barnehurst.
7.18 a.m. to Addiscombe.
7.54 a.m. to Addiscombe.
8. 3 a.m. to Slade Green.
8.38 a.m. to Addiscombe.
10. 6 a.m. to Barnehurst.
10.31 a.m. to Addiscombe.
12.10 p.m. to Dartford (Pcls.).
4. 2 p.m. to Crayford.
4.24 p.m. to Bromley North.
4.27 p.m. to Dartford.
4.46½ p.m. to Selsdon.
5. 1 p.m. to Sanderstead.
5.24 p.m. to Plumstead.
6.29½ p.m. to Bromley North.
6.55 p.m. to New Beckenham.
8.27 p.m. to Plumstead.

From Addiscombe.
5.57 a.m. to Charing Cross.
7.39 a.m. to Cannon Street.
8. 1 a.m. to Cannon Street.
9.14 a.m. to Cannon Street.
2.51 p.m. to Hayes.
3.30 p.m. to Cannon Street.
6. 6 p.m. to Cannon Street.
7.13 p.m. to Elmers End.

From Barnehurst.
6.53 a.m. to Holborn Vdt.
7.13 a.m. to Charing Cross.
4.46 p.m. to Holborn Vdt.

From Bellingham.
5.14 p.m. to Blackfriars.

From Bickley.
7.33 a.m. to Holborn Vdt.
8.32 a.m. to Holborn Vdt.
6.20 p.m. to Holborn Vdt.

From Charing Cross.
6.40 a.m. to Barnehurst.
7. 3 a.m. to Bromley North
8. 4 a.m. to Dartford.
4.36 p.m. to Addiscombe.
6.12 p.m. to Sanderstead.
6.25 p.m. to Addiscombe.

From Bromley North.
6.26 a.m. to Cannon Street.
5. 1 p.m. to Cannon Street
8.22 p.m. to Cannon Street.

From Dartford.
3.29 p.m. to Cannon Street.

From Gravesend Central.
6.48 a.m. to Cannon Street.

From Hayes.
11.20 a.m. to Addiscombe.
3.59 p.m. to Charing Cross.
8. 6 p.m. to Elmers End.

From New Beckenham.
2.48 p.m. to Cannon Street.

From Orpington.
6. 6 a.m. to Holborn Vdt.
6.25 a.m. to Holborn Vdt.
5.47 p.m. to Holborn Vdt.

From Blackfriars.
7.58 a.m. to Wimbledon.
5.27 p.m. to Bellingham.
6. 6 p.m. to Bellingham
6.10 p.m. to Barnehurst.
6.59 p.m. to Bellingham.

From Holborn Viaduct.
6.43 a.m. to Orpington.
7.28 a.m. to Orpington.
7.44 a.m. to Bickley.
8. 6 a.m. to Bickley.
9.14 a.m. to Loughborough († Sdgs.).
9.25 a.m. to Bellingham.
10.29 a.m. to Wimbledon.
3.47 p.m. to Orpington.
5.27 p.m. to Orpington.
6.27 p.m. to Bickley.
6.47 p.m. to Orpington.

From Plumstead.
5.48 a.m. to Cannon Street.
6. 1 p.m. to Cannon Street.

From St. Helier.
8. 7 a.m. to Blackfriars.

From Sanderstead.
6.25 a.m. to Cannon Street.
7.23 a.m. to Charing Cross.
5.47 p.m. to Charing Cross.

From Selsdon.
5.29 p.m. to Charing Cross.

From Slade Green.
6.44 a.m. to Charing Cross.

From Wimbledon.
8.40 a.m. to Holborn Vdt.

Ice and Snow

The last pages of the fog notices included the requirements for the working of de-icing trains. Snow and ice could be just as disruptive, and of course falling snow was just as bad as fog for reducing visibility, and needed to be dealt with similarly. Ice forming on the conductor rail was especially difficult to deal with, so an oil-based fluid was spread on to the head of the rail to try and prevent freezing, applied from specially adapted carriages marshalled in special empty electric trains that ran over predetermined routes. In 1945 some of the ex-LBSCR trailer carriages from withdrawn two-car trailer sets were gutted and equipped with tanks and a control position from which de-icing fluid could be squirted on to the top of the conductor rail. The first batch were numbered DS351 to DS356 (351S to 356S in SR days), later joined by Nos DS396 to DS399. Not being self-propelled, these had to be sandwiched between two suburban motor units, and therefore retained their through power, light and control jumpers. In 1960 some of the recently withdrawn motor coaches from the 1925 Metropolitan Vickers units were converted to self-propelled de-icing units. These were given unit numbers S92 to S101, but for operation over the newly electrified area in East Kent three ex-4SUB all-steel trailers was converted to de-icing trailers but with EPB jumpers to allow them to work between units with EPB control gear.

One of the worst conditions to tackle was 'black ice'. During cold weather rain falling on the conductor rail would wash off any de-icing fluid, and if the temperature of the rail was at or below freezing point the rain would then form a thin film of ice. Ice is an excellent electrical insulator. Early electric trains had gravity shoes to collect current; these were of cast iron suspended on flexible links from the shoe beam, and had ends that sloped up to ease passage over gaps in the rail. If a layer of ice formed, they would ride over it and lose contact. From the 1950s a type of spring-loaded shoe was fitted, which had a vertical plough face at either end intended to cut through snow, but it could not always be relied upon to break up black ice. Various means of breaking the ice have been considered, including scraper brushes with wire bristles, and even heating the conductor rail, but none have been truly successful.

In addition to the problem of ice on the conductor rail, snow and ice can severely hamper the operation of junctions. Snow will drift between point blades and become compressed, preventing them from closing properly, thus preventing a safe passage for a train. Salt has been used, but its corrosive effects can be severely damaging to track components and signalling

The snowploughs converted from former 'Schools' Class steam locomotive tenders are seen here during conversion at Eastleigh. *Mark Abbott*

De-icing units

Unit No	Departmental coach No	Former passenger No	Former set No
92	DS70044 (DS70173)	S8456S (S8457S)	4345
92	DS70045	S8455S	4345
93	DS70090	S8446S	4340
93	DS70091	S8445S	4340
94	DS70092	S8463S	4349
94	DS70093	S8464S	4349
95	DS70094	S8453S	4344
95	DS70095	S8454S	4344
96	DS70096	S8433S	4334
96	DS70097	S8434S	4334
97	DS70098	S8471S	4353
97	DS70099	S8472S	4553
98	DS70100	S8476S	4351
98	DS70101	S8468S	4351
99	DS70102	S8422S	4328
99	DS70103	S8421S	4328
100	DS70104	S8430S	4332
100	DS70105	S8465S	4332
101	DS70106	S8427S	4331
101	DS70107	S8423S	4331
Single vehicle	DS70050	S10392S	4345
Single vehicle	DS70051	S10399S	4351
Single vehicle	DS70087	S10400S	4349

apparatus. Manual scraping was once the most regular means of keeping points in operation, but this can be labour-intensive and carries risks to the permanent way staff undertaking the work. Too many platelayers have been struck and killed by trains over the years while attending to frozen points. De-icing fluid can be used, but this also requires manual application. The safest and most practical method for keeping these areas free of ice and snow is to fit the point switches with heaters. In the 1960s many key junctions were heated by bottled propane gas, kept in lineside cages or compounds and connected to the heaters by pipes, but even so the heaters needed to be lit manually. Later automatic ignition was provided using a thermostatic switch to operate a spark plug. The latest technique is to use electric heaters strapped to the rails.

Manual signalling can also be seriously affected by ice, and although the signalman was instructed in the Rule Book to operate his equipment frequently to prevent it freezing, the assistance of the Permanent Way Department was frequently needed. Mechanical signalling is designed to 'fail safe' even if snow and ice affects it, but there were occasions when signal arms froze in the 'clear' position. Fortunately most signals are indicated back to the signalman, who should investigate any signal showing 'wrong' on his indicator and not responding to the lever. He should then take steps to protect the line until the signal is working properly. Drivers were specially advised

in the Sectional Appendix to reduce speed when encountering lower-quadrant signals at clear during snow storms, and to treat the distant as a caution at all times.

Colour light signalling could also be affected by the build-up of snow on the lens hood, obscuring the aspect of the light above. For this reason the red 'stop' aspect is always the lowest one of a group. This has not always been the case, and early Southern Railway four-aspect signals would place the second yellow below the red. This practice has now been discontinued.

The South East is usually regarded as a place of mild weather, but the East and North Kent coasts can be badly affected by weather coming in from the North Sea. Faversham and Ashford depots had snowploughs allocated at various times. In 1949 Ramsgate and Ashford were each allocated a peculiar double-ended snow plough, similar to some built by the North Eastern Railway. Numbered S3 and S4, they were built at Ashford to drawings prepared at Eastleigh, following on from two produced in 1929 (respectively Nos S1 and S2) for Basingstoke and Salisbury. These were not popular with the Locomotive Department: they did not accommodate staff, who therefore needed to ride on the locomotive, and they had a peculiar collapsible buffer beam incorporated in the plough that needed to be raised at the pushing end and dropped at the ploughing end before they could be moved. Fortunately the number of occasions each year that they were actually

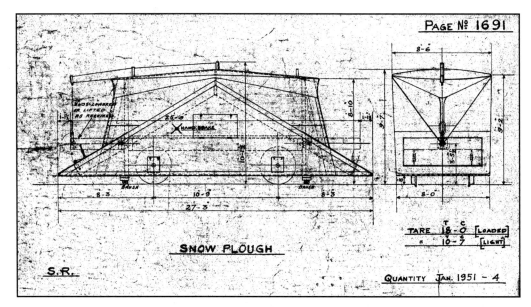

Diagram 1691 for the double-ended snowplough.

'C' Class 0-6-0 No 31112 at Faversham shed in 1963, fitted with a snowplough. *Author's collection*

required was negligible. Later, about ten Wainwright Class 'C' 0-6-0 locomotives were fitted with buffer-beam snowploughs each winter and kept in readiness at various South Eastern and Central division sheds. In 1957 some of these were also fitted with conductor rail ice-scraping gear attached to shoe beams fixed to their tenders. These would run at night to keep the 'juice rail' clear. In December 1961 two Class 'Cs', Nos 31112 and 31268, were fitted with large nose-end ploughs, which completely covered the front of the smokebox, and were stationed at Faversham until the following March. Nos 31271, 31280 and 31592 were similarly fitted and observed at Ashford the following year (see 'SW14'). The fate of the double-ended ploughs is not known. Independent ploughs did not appear until about 1964 when eight Class 'V' tenders were converted to snow ploughs by Eastleigh works and distributed around the region. Details of these are given in the accompanying table.

Snowploughs converted from Class 'V' tenders

Number	Former tender number	Location in 1980
DS70210	723	Ashford
DS70211	731	Ashford
DS70224	739	Eastleigh
DS70225	715	Redhill
DS70226	701	Salisbury
DS70227	729	Salisbury
DS70228	734	Eastleigh
DS70229	735	Redhill

Addition to Notice headed:—

'Working of Trains during Fog, Ice and Snow'

also

'Running of De-Icing Trains
Winter 1957/1958 and until further notice'

London East Publication   page 11 item 25
London Central Publication   page 15 item 26
London West Publication   page 13 item 25

Add:—

The following Westinghouse fitted steam locomotives have been furnished with brackets for the purpose of attaching Conductor Rail Ice-Scraping Equipment which will be mounted at the Motive Power Depots on the occasions required for service as scrapers:—

Motive Power Depot	Engine Nos.	
Bricklayers Arms	31717	
Brighton	31724	31725
Gillingham	31720	
Guildford	31722	31723
Hither Green	31721	
Stewarts Lane	31719	

These engines will be provided by the Motive Power Depot concerned on due notice from the District Central Office stating the route to be covered.

Apart from the connection from the above-mentioned Motive Power Depots to the electrified running lines the engines with the Ice-Scraper Equipment mounted must be confined to electrified running lines and must not be permitted to run or shunt on non-electrified lines nor on sidings, electrified or otherwise.

The engines performing the scraping will run 'light' and will operate with the current on or off the conductor rail.

(P/EW 4, L.C.D. 1958)

(T/EP.4)
(G.1592.R.)
(L.4052/TP.) (2)

De-Icer 93 seen here at Fratton on 18th April 1964 was created from the motor coaches of former Southern Railway 1926 Metropolitan Carriage and Wagon built suburban unit 4540 (Motor coach numbers S8546S and S8645S renumbered on conversion DS70090 and DS70091 respectively). Inside each carriage the seating had been removed and replaced with a de-icing fluid tank and controls to distribute the oily liquid through pipes to additional 'shoe' beams on the trailing bogies. Ice scrapers and brushes were also provided to remove snow and ice before the oil was applied. *The Southern Way*

II

24. WORKING OF TRAINS UNDER CONDITIONS OF ICE OR SNOW.

The following are the conditions of Ice or Snow on the conductor rails which render the running of trains difficult :—

(a) Ice frozen on to rails either in small patches close together or continuous glazing.   (b) Heavy hoar frost.

(c) Snow frozen on to rails.   (d) Snow covering rails.

---

25. SNOW AND ICE SCRAPERS.

All 4-car lavatory units and certain 2-car " Bil " units are fitted with pneumatically operated ice and snow scrapers mounted on either motor bogie or driving trailer bogie shoe beams. The de-icing trains used for depositing a protective fluid on the conductor rail are similarly equipped. The scrapers are suitable for use at speeds not exceeding 60 m.p.h., and can be lowered or raised, to scrape or not, from the cab over the bogie, which is fitted with them. Motormen are instructed to lower them to scrape the conductor rail whenever experiencing difficulty in current collection due to snow and ice conditions, and to raise them clear immediately after the need for their use has passed, so as to avoid unnecessary wear of the scrapers.

Operating Department staff at stations and depots at which electric stock is berthed should do their best to ensure that, so far as is possible, units fitted with ice scrapers are sent out on the first services over the various routes whenever ice or snow is present or expected.

Where possible the first Up Train from Gillingham and Maidstone East and West, to be formed of stock fitted with ice scrapers.

26. RUNNING OF SPECIAL DE-ICING TRAINS.

When required, a service of special De-icing trains will be run in order to keep the conductor rails clear of ice or snow. The special De-icing trains may be formed of either :—
(1) A two-coach De-icing electric unit
or
(2) A De-icing coach fitted with hand brake.
The special De-icing trains are allocated to the following depots :—

27. LONDON EAST DISTRICT.

Gillingham (Kent) ... ...   2 De-icing coaches.

28. LONDON CENTRAL DISTRICT

Selhurst ... ...   I De-icing coach.
Brighton ... ...   2 De-icing coaches.

29. LONDON WEST DISTRICT.

Wimbledon Park Sidings... ... ...   I two-coach De-icing electric unit.
                          I De-icing coach.
Fratton ... ...   I two-coach De-icing electric unit.
The two-coach De-icing electric units work independently, and can, if required, be attached to ordinary electric services (express train stock and E.P.B. excepted).

The De-icing coach may be formed between any four two-car units or two four-car old type suburban units (two-car units to be used when possible), but if stock is not available the De-icing coach may be formed with one unit at each end Express train stock and E.P.B. must **not** be used.

A member of the Electrical Engineer's Staff will travel with each De-icing coach or De-icing Electric Unit to regulate supply of fluid to the Conductor Rail.
It is important that these trains keep strictly to the routes shown.
These trains must be returned to their respective Depots.
These services are to be signalled as empty passenger trains.
De-icing trains will be referred to by their Table Numbers.
Motormen and Guards to be rostered to work the De-icing trains as from Monday, 4th November, 1957, until Saturday, 29th March, 1958 inclusive.

30. Weather Reports.—(a) **The Station Masters at Gillingham, Swanley, Wrotham, Maidstone East, Sevenoaks, Orpington, Grove Park, Dartford, Charlton, Eltham (W.H.), Sidcup, Elmers End, Shortlands and Nunhead** must, in the event of the conductor rails becoming affected by frost, ice or snow, after 5.0 p.m., at once ascertain whether similar conditions exist at stations or signal boxes in the immediate neighbourhood and advise Orpington Control, who will then transmit the information to the Electrical Control, London Bridge (Extn. 2770) not later than 6.0 p.m., who will decide as to the necessity or otherwise of running the special de-icing trains.

Pending the decision the Station Masters at the stations affected must await instructions as to whether signal boxes will require to be kept open specially for the running of the de-icing trains.

(b) Electrical Control, London Bridge, will order out trains as necessary.

(c) The frost may be of such nature that it does not cause serious interference with the conductor rail, and the Electrical Control will bear this in mind when coming to a decision as to the running of the trains, but similar conditions may arise after the trains are running ; the District Traffic Control will obtain reports and advise the Electrical Control in order that a decision to continue or withdraw the trains may be made.

Unless instructions are received to the contrary the trains when ordered out will complete their rostered circuit.

Lond. East Fog Supp.—3

RUNNING OF SPECIAL DE-ICING TRAINS—*continued.*

(d) If ice has already formed on the conductor rail it may be necessary to use a steam locomotive, preferably Westinghouse Brake fitted, to haul the de-icing trains. If this is not possible, such trains will work as a freight train and the Guard must ride in the rear vehicle which must be fitted with a hand brake.

    If necessary, the special coach may be attached to the steam locomotive, the guard riding in this coach which is fitted with a hand brake. In such cases the attachment of electric train units is not required.

(e) In addition to the foregoing arrangements, additional units may require to be attached to certain early morning services as ordered by the Electrical Control, London Bridge, in order to increase the number of shoes. District Traffic Controls to arrange as directed.

(f) In the event of extremely severe weather conditions being experienced it may be necessary to run electric trains during the night on sections of the line not covered by the de-icing trains. These trains will operate on request of Electrical Control, London Bridge, to the District Traffic Controls.

(g) It may be necessary on occasion to order out a 2-coach de-icing electric unit or the Special Coach or a unit fitted with scrapers for the purpose of clearing snow from the conductor rail only, in which case **Orpington Control** may do so without further authority from the Electrical Control, London Bridge. For the purpose of advices, these will be referred to as **"Snow Scraping Trains."**

(h) The Electrical Control at London Bridge will advise at 8.0 a.m. and 3.0 p.m. whether it is advisable to break down the formation of the trains as shown in Carriage Working Notices.

31. Engineering Work.—Ballast, Material or Stone Trains.—The running of ballast, material, etc., trains in connection with the carrying out of Engineering Works, under icing conditions, will continue as notified, provided the working of the special trains run for preventing the formation of ice and snow on the conductor rails will not be interfered with thereby. The District Engineer will arrange for communication to be maintained between the Signal Box controlling entry to the section and the site of the work so that ballast, etc., trains may be cleared, or the Engineering work be suspended and the electric current be restored at short notice as required.

32.   One Coach stabled at Gillingham will run in the following schedule :—

	Week-days and Suns.	SX	SO	Sun.		Week-days and Suns.	SX	SO	Sun.
Table	21	22	23	24	Table	21	22	23	24
Headcode	27	54	54	54	Headcode	27	54	54	54
	a.m.	p.m.	p.m.	p.m.		a.m.	p.m.	p.m.	p.m.
Gillingham ... dep.	2 20	7 25	6 46	7 40	St. Mary Cray Jn. ...	...	11/25	11/25	11/51
Chatham	2/23	7/29	6/50	7/43	Bickley Jn.	...	11/26	11/26M	11/52M
Rochester Bridge ...	2/26	7/34	6/53	7/46	Bromley South { arr.	...	11 29	11 29	11 55
Sole Street	2/42	7/46	7/ 3	7/56					night
Swanley ... { arr.	2 54	7 59	7 14	8 7	{ dep.	...	11 38	11 38M	12 8M
{ dep.	3 0	8 8	7 23	8 14	Bickley Jn.	...	11/41	11/41	12/11
Otford	3/11	8/17	7/34	8/25	St. Mary Cray Jn. ...	...	11/42	11/42	12/12
Wrotham	3/18	8/23	7/40	8/31	Swanley ... { arr.	4 10	11 49	11 49	...
Maidstone East { arr.	3 32	8 35	7 52	8 43	{ dep.	4 20	11 54	11 54	12/17
{ dep.	3 40	8 40	8 7	9 14			night	night	
Wrotham ... { arr.	...	...	8 20	...	Sole Street	4/35	12/12	12/12	12/27
{ dep.	3/54	8/54	8 27	9/28	Cuxton Road Box ...	4/41	12/16	12/16	12/32
Otford ... { arr.	...	9 11	8 35	9 34	Rochester Bridge Jn.	4/48	12/18	12/18	12/35½
{ dep.	...	9 16	8 40	9 39	Rochester { arr.	...	12 20	12 20	12 37
Sevenoaks ... { arr.	...	9 22	8 46	9 45	{ dep.	...	12 25	12 25	12 42
{ dep.	...	9 27	9 24	9 55	Strood ... ... { arr.	...	12 28	12 28	12 45
Orpington ... { arr.	...	9 39	9 38	10 9	{ dep.	...	12 33	12 33	12 50
{ dep.	...	10 40	10 40	11 10	Maidstone West { arr.	...	12 58	12 58	1 10
Sevenoaks ... { arr.	...	10 57	10 57	11 24	{ dep.	...	1 20	1 5	1 15
{ dep.	...	11 2	11 2	11 29	Strood ... ... { arr.	...	1 50	1 25	1 35
Otford	...	11/8	11/8	11/33	{ dep.	...	1 55	1 30	1 40
Swanley ... { arr.	4 10	...	...	...	Rochester Bridge Jn. ...	...	1/57	1/32	1/42
{ dep.	4 20	11/20	11/20	11/45	Chatham	4/54	2/ 0	1/35	1/45
					Gillingham ... arr.	4 58	2 4	1 40	1 49

13

RUNNING OF SPECIAL DE-ICING TRAINS—continued.

33.   **One Coach** stabled at Gillingham (Kent), will run in the following schedule :—

Table	7	8	9
Headcode	53	53	53
	SX	SO	Suns.
	p.m.	p.m.	p.m.
Gillingham... ... dep.	8 14	8 14	8 14
Chatham ... ... ,,	8/19	8/19	8/19
Rochester Bridge Jn. ,,	8/23	8/23	8/23
Sole Street ... ... ,,	8/38	8/38	8/38
Swanley... ... ... ,,	8/55	8/55	8/55
St. Mary Cray Jn. ,,	9/ 1	9/ 1	9/ 1
Bickley Jn. ... ... ,,	9/ 2ML	9/ 2ML	9/ 2ML
Beckenham Jn. ... ,,	9/ 7	9/ 7	9/ 7
Herne Hill ... { arr.	9 16	9 16	9 16
dep.	9 21DN	9 21DN	9 21DN
arr.	10 50DN	10 50DN	11 11DN
dep.	11 0	11 0	11 18
Beckenham Jn. ... ,,	11/ 8	11/ 8	11/28
Shortlands	11/11LL	11/11LL	11/31LL
Bickley ... ... { arr.	11 15LL	11 15LL	11 35LL
dep.	11 23LL	11 23LL	11 42LL
Shortlands ... { arr.	11 27LL	11 27LL	11 48LL
dep.	11 36ML	11 36ML	11 53ML
Bickley Jn. ... ... ,,	11/42	11/42	11/58
			mdt.
Orpington ... { arr.	11 47TL	11 47TL	12 4TL
	mdt.	mdt.	...
dep.	12 0LL	12 0LL	12 9LL
Chislehurst	12/ 4	12/ 4	12/14
Grove Park ... { arr.	12 8LL	12 8LL	12 18LL
dep.	12 20LL	12 20LL	12 23LL
Chislehurst ... ... ,,	12/25	12/25	12/30
Orpington ... { arr.	12 30LL	12 30LL	12 36LL
dep.	12 35	12 35	12 41
Bickley Jn. ... ... ,,	12/40	12/40	12/46
Bickley ... ... { arr.	12 42	12 42	12 48
dep.	12 47	12 47	12 53
Bickley Jn. ... ... ,,	12/48	12/48	12/54
St. Mary Cray Jn.... ,,	12/49	12/49	12/56
Swanley...	12/54	12/54	1/ 0
Sole Street ... ... ,,	1/ 6	1/ 6	1/12
Rochester Bridge Jn. ,,	1/15	1/15	1/22
Chatham	1/18	1/18	1/25
Gillingham... ... arr.	1 22	1 22	1 28

October, 1957.

WORKING OF SPECIAL DE-ICING TRAINS.

36. The following are the conditions of Ice or Snow on the conductor rails which render the running of trains difficult :—

(a) Ice frozen on to rails either in small patches close together or continuous glazing.
(b) Heavy hoar frost.
(c) Snow frozen on to rails.
(d) Snow covering rails.

When required a service of special de-icing trains as shown herein will be run in order to keep the conductor rails clear of ice or snow.

De-icing coaches fitted with hand brakes will be available for use and allocated for service as under. These coaches may be formed between any four 2-car units or two 4-car units (2-car units to be used when possible) but if stock is not available the de-icing coach may be formed with one unit at each end. **Express train Stock must not be used.**

An Electrical Engineer's man will travel with each de-icing coach to regulate supply of fluid to the Conductor rail.

One Coach stabled at Gillingham, will run in the following schedule :—

	S.X.	S.O.	Sun.			S.X.	S.O.	Sun.
	p.m.	p.m.	p.m.			p.m.	p.m.	p.m.
Gillingham ... ...dep.	7 36	6 46	7 38	Otford	11/24	10/41	11/24
Chatham...	7/40	6/50	7/41	Swanley	11/36	10/53	11/36
Rochester Bridge Jc.	7/45	6/53	7/44	St. Mary Cray Jc....	11/42	10/58	11/42
Sole Street	7/56	7/ 3	7/54	Bickley Jc.	11/43M	10/59M	11/43M
Swanley ... ... { arr.	8 7	7 13	8 4	Bromley South ... { arr.	11 46	11 1	11 46
{ dep.	8 23	7 23	8 14	{ dep.	11 52M	11 12M	11 52M
Otford	8/33	7/34	8/25	Bickley Jc.	11/55	11/15	11/55
Wrotham	8/39	7/40	8/31	St. Mary Cray Jc....	11/56	11/16	11/56
Maidstone East ... { arr.	8 51	7 52	8 43	Swanley	12/ 1	11/22	12/ 1
{ dep.	8 56	8 7	9 14	Sole Street	12/11	11/36	12/11
Wrotham ... ... { arr.	...	8 20	...	Cuxton Road...	12/16	11/41	12/16
{ dep.	9/15	8 27	9/28	Rochester Bridge Jc.	12/19½	11/45	12/19½
Otford ... ... { arr.	9 24	8 35	9 34	Rochester ... ... { arr.	12 21	11 47	12 21
{ dep.	9 35	8 40	9 39	{ dep.	12 27	11 52	12 27
Sevenoaks ... ... { arr.	9 41	8 45	9 45	Strood ... ... { arr.	12 31	11 55	12 31
{ dep.	10 14	9 24	9 55	{ dep.	12 49	12 0	12 40
Orpington ... ... { arr.	10 25	9 35	10 6	Maidstone West ... { arr.	1 21	12 20	1 0
{ dep.	11 2	10 16	10 51	{ dep.	1 28	12 26	1 7
Sevenoaks ... ... { arr.	11 13	10 27	11 2	Strood ... ... { arr.	1 48	12 46	1 27
{ dep.	11 20	10 35	11 20	{ dep.	1 54	1 5	1 34
				Rochester Bridge Jc.	1/56	1/ 7	1/36
				Chatham...	1/59	1/10	1/39
				Gillingham ... ... arr.	2 4	1 15	1 44

It is important these trains keep strictly to the routes shown.
These trains must be returned to Gillingham.
These services to be signalled as empty passenger trains.

Speed.—The speed of these trains **must not exceed 60 miles per hour,** but all Restrictions which impose a slower speed must be observed.

Motormen & Guards to be rostered to work the de-icing trains as from Monday, 3rd November, 1952.

Weather Reports.—(a) **The Station Masters at Gillingham, Swanley, Maidstone East, Sevenoaks, Orpington, Grove Park, Dartford, Charlton, Eltham (W.H.), Sidcup, Elmers End, Shortlands and Nunhead** must, in the event of the conductor rails becoming affected by frost, ice or snow, after 5.0 p.m., at

72

WORKING OF SPECIAL DE-ICING TRAINS UNDER CONDITIONS OF ICE OR SNOW—*contd.*

once ascertain whether similar conditions exist at stations or signal boxes in the immediate neighbourhood and advise Orpington Control, who will then transmit the information to the Electrical Engineer's Control, London Bridge (Extn. 2770) not later than 6.0 p.m., who will decide as to the necessity or otherwise of running the special de-icing trains.

Pending the decision the Station Masters at the stations affected must await instructions as to whether signal boxes will require to be kept open specially for the running of the de-icing trains.

(b) Electrical Engineer's Control, London Bridge, will order out trains as necessary.

(c) The frost may be of such nature that it does not cause interference with the conductor rail, and the Electrical Engineers' Control will bear this in mind when coming to a decision as to the running of the trains, but similar conditions may arise after the trains are running; the Divisional Traffic Control will obtain reports and advise the Electrical Engineers' Control in order that a decision to continue or withdraw the trains may be made.

Unless instructions are received to the contrary the trains when ordered out will complete their rostered circuit.

(d) If ice has already formed on the conductor rail it may be necessary to use a steam locomotive to haul the de-icing trains. Engines equipped with the Westinghouse brake will be provided. If this is not possible such trains will work as a freight train and the Guard must ride in the rear vehicle which must be fitted with a hand brake.

If necessary, the special coach may be attached to the steam locomotive, the guard riding in this coach which is fitted with a hand brake. In such cases the attachment of electric train units is not required.

(e) In addition to the foregoing arrangements, additional units may require to be attached to certain early morning services as ordered by the Electrical Engineer's Control, London Bridge, in order to increase the number of shoes. Divisional Traffic Controls to arrange as directed.

(f) In the event of extremely severe weather conditions being experienced it may be necessary to run electric trains during the night on sections of the line not covered by the de-icing trains. These trains will operate on request of Electrical Engineer's Control, London Bridge, to the Divisional Traffic Controls.

(g) The Electrical Engineer's Control at London Bridge will advise at 8.0 a.m. and 5.0 p.m. whether it is advisable to break down the formation of the trains as shown in Carriage Working Notices. In the absence of an advice to the contrary trains will be reduced in formation as normally.

(h) Where possible the first Up Train from Gillingham & Maidstone, East & West, to be formed of stock fitted with ice scrapers.

Engineering Work.—Ballast, Material or Stone Trains.—The running of ballast, material, etc., trains in connection with the carrying out of Engineer's Works, under conditions of ice and snow, will continue as notified provided the working of the special trains run for preventing the formation of ice and snow on the conductor rails will not be interfered with thereby. The Divisional Engineer will arrange for communication to be maintained between the Signal Box controlling entry to the section and the site of the work so that ballast, etc., trains may be cleared, or the Engineering work be suspended and the electric current be restored at short notice as required.

McCorquodale, London, S.E.—2960

Flooding and Landslips

Flooding in East Kent,
1 February 1953

These floods were discussed in detail in 'Southern Way' No 13 in 2011 and were undoubtedly one of the most serious disasters to affect the railways of the South East since the war. Fortunately in East Kent it happened with no loss of life, although sadly the same could not be said elsewhere because the floods affected many parts of Eastern Britain as well as Holland.

Briefly, a storm surge in the North Sea added to an exceptional high tide exceeded the planned defences and overtopped the sea and estuary defences along the coast of Kent, breaching them in several places and washing away the railway lines near the coasts. Worst affected were Reculver between Herne Bay and Birchington, Graveney between Faversham and Whitstable, the Isle of Sheppey, Strood and Belvedere. It was not until May that services returned to normal on all routes. Work involved in restoring the railway included a new chalk embankment and sea wall between Herne Bay and Birchington, which necessitated a day and night service of goods trains carrying chalk from quarries near Knockholt and also near Margate. A temporary spur line was laid at Canterbury to allow trains to climb up from the Ramsgate to Ashford line to the Dover to Faversham line. A gruesome duty for the Southern breakdown gang during this clear up was to recover the carcases of drowned cattle that had been washed on to the track on the Sheerness branch.

The sea wall between Reculver and Birchington can be seen breached in the distance on 2 February 1953. The photographer is standing on the railway embankment with the water lapping at his feet, showing the distance that the water has travelled to the railway.

A concrete permanent way hut has floated on the incoming tide and now rests on the track near Birchington on the same day.

The track at Birchington is distorted, swept aside by the tide. It should in fact extend straight ahead, and the ballast has been washed away.

Another view of the washed-out railway at Birchington on 2 February 1953.

Storm damage, 5 September 1958

This time it was rain and not the tides that wreaked havoc. On the evening of Friday 5 September 1958 at about 7.00pm a terrific storm struck Southern England. The routes from London into Kent were breached in numerous places.

One of the worst hit places was St Mary Cray, where a deep hole 50 feet deep by 12 feet square appeared under an embankment recently widened as part of the Kent Coast scheme. At Sevenoaks landslips blocked the main line at both ends of the tunnel. The water had rushed through the 2-mile-long tunnel and carried sleepers and rubble with it.

The suburban area also suffered a lot of damage. At least twenty earth slips occurred on the Bexleyheath line alone. Fortunately these were fairly minor and the line reopened at 4.30am on Saturday 6th. In fact, that line was the only route available into Kent via Chatham on the Saturday morning.

Single-line working was put in operation between Redhill and Tonbridge at 8.00am on Saturday, giving access over the South Eastern main line as far as Ashford.

The hole in the new embankment at St Mary Cray opened by excessive rainfall in September 1958.

Looking southwards out of Sevenoaks Tunnel after the embankment slip.

An embankment slip at the south end of Sevenoaks Tunnel, also in September 1958.

Further serious landslips during Friday evening occurred at or between Blackheath and Charlton, Erith and Slade Green, Blackheath and Kidbrooke, New Eltham, New Eltham and Sidcup, Sidcup and Albany Park, Crayford and Bexley, Greenhithe, Gravesend Central, St Mary Cray, Fawkham, Fawkham and Sole Street, Shoreham, Otford and Bat & Ball, Bat & Ball and Sevenoaks, Sevenoaks and Weald, Dunton Green and Polhill, and Dunton Green and Chevening Halt.

Flooding occurred at Clock House (New Beckenham and Elmers End), where water reached a depth of 2 feet in the station, as well as at Blackheath, Woolwich Dockyard and Beckenham Hill..

Permanent way teams worked round the clock to carry our repairs, and by Monday 8 September all routes were reopened except the Westerham branch.

Storm and flooding, 14/15 September 1968

Ten years later it all happened again when storms caused chaos in the South East of England during Saturday and Sunday 14 and 15 September 1968. Reported as the heaviest rainstorm of the century, many towns were flooded when numerous rivers, swollen by the torrential downpour, burst their banks. It rained continuously from Saturday until Sunday evening. In West Sussex a tornado was reported, and a whirlwind reported to be 100 yards wide appears also to have struck Hoo, Wainscott and Chattenden on the Medway estuary, ripping roofs off about forty houses. Damage and flooding were also reported throughout the Home Counties.

Railways suffered badly and for a time on Sunday there were no routes open at all between London and Kent. The Medway, Cray, Eden and Darenth rivers all overtopped their banks, Dartford, Westerham, Tonbridge and Edenbridge towns were badly flooded, and many places were cut off. The Bexleyheath line embankment at Bellgrove Road, Welling, collapsed. Between

Kemsing and Borough Green 60 feet of track was washed away. A cutting side-slipped at Hildenborough and blocked the line. All the electrical signalling failed at Tonbridge because it was under water. The rain also caused surface water flooding in countless places because the drainage was unable to cope.

Lines closed by the flooding included the Catford Loop, Dartford Loop, Mid Kent, Borough Green to Kemsing, Otford to Sevenoaks, Sevenoaks to Tonbridge, Tonbridge to Redhill, Lenham to Maidstone East, Maidstone and Aylesford (a bus service was provided). The Bexleyheath line provided a restricted service. A train was disabled at Edenbridge by flood water and eighty passengers had to be evacuated. Sanderstead signal box was struck by lightning, and an electric train near Barnehurst was also struck.

Repair work to restore services was originally estimated to require two or three days, but all train services on the South Eastern Division were restored, with some speed reduction, by Monday.

Clock House station is seen here in dry weather in 1945. After heavy rain the space between the platforms would fill with water overflowing from the Poole River to the north of the station. In steam days the service was maintained by a train of steam stock 'topped and tailed' by steam locomotives between Lower Sydenham and Addiscombe.

Flooding at Clock House

One point on the South Eastern was regularly flooded every winter, and occasionally in the summer too if a thunderstorm passed nearby. The River Poole, a tributary of the Ravensbourne, passes under the Mid Kent line just north of Clock House station between New Beckenham and Elmers End. After periods of heavy rain the river frequently rose to a point where it overtopped the bridge (No 683) and started to flow down the track into Clock House station, eventually filling the trackbed between the platforms above conductor rail level. Trains were permitted to run at no more than 3mph until the water level reached a danger mark, when special instructions were to be implemented. The mark consisted of an arrow painted on a board fixed to the down-side abutment of the station footbridge (No 685). As soon as the water reached this mark, the train service was normally suspended and passengers directed to use local buses. The Electrical Control Room at Lewisham would monitor the current, which was to be switched off as soon as the water reached the conductor rail.

The problem with electric traction is that water can conduct electricity. Current leakage from the third rail, if it is in contact with water, causes excessive electrical loss, and may

Steam haulage of passenger stock through floodwater at Clock House was no longer practicable after steam was abolished on the South Eastern Division in 1962, but in 1964 a pair of BRCW/Sulzer Type 3 Bo-Bo locomotives (one seen here) were experimentally equipped with waterproofing to the traction motors to haul a train of EPB electric stock. This experiment does not appear to have been satisfactory, and bus substitution remained the order of the day until the Poole River was finally enclosed in a concrete culvert, which appears to have cured the problem.

in fact increase the risk of damage to nearby signalling and telecommunication systems. There is also a risk of electric shock to any person in contact with water that is touching the conductor rail. Electric trains passing through water will throw water into the electrical parts of the traction motors, risking short circuits and 'flashovers'. The same also applies to diesel-electric locomotives that have traction motors on the bogies.

To keep the service going, from time to time a shuttle service of steam-hauled coaches would be implemented between Lower Sydenham and Addiscombe. Steam locomotives are generally better at coping with brief encounters with flood water. However, with the abolition of steam in Kent in 1961 that option was removed. In 1964 trials took place with Type 3 diesel-electrics with specially protected traction equipment, although it does not appear to have been an overwhelming success.

The Poole River has now been covered in a concrete culvert and in recent years flooding has rarely occurred.

Strood Tunnel

The line between Higham and Strood is built on the filled-in bed of the old Thames & Medway Canal. As the line emerges from the tunnel it turns right into Strood station alongside the former canal basin, and here the tracks are only a few feet above the level of the River Medway. At times of high water after heavy rain coupled with a high tide, water can enter the tunnel and, if high enough, will flood the tunnel and require electric traffic to be stopped. That is not the only problem, however: both Higham and Strood tunnels were unlined, having been simply cut through the native chalk. Falls of chalk were therefore a frequent occurrence and, if large enough, would also obstruct the tunnel; large falls could block the line for weeks at a time. As a precaution telephones were provided, connected to the signal boxes at either end, and in an emergency one long ring on the telephone circuit was sufficient to stop traffic.

Folkestone to Dover

Damage to the railway on the stretch of the South Eastern route between Folkestone and Dover has been a headache to the railway authorities for as long as the route has been in existence, and continues to be so. The incidents on 28 November 1939, when 25,000 tons of chalk cliff collapsed, and again in February 1940, have already been discussed in 'SW8'. The chalk cliffs hereabouts are notoriously unstable and the fall in 1915 actually derailed a train and took a considerable length of time to clear.

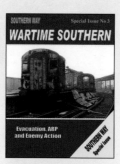
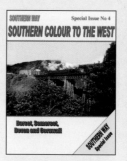

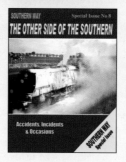
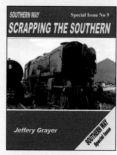
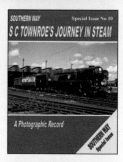
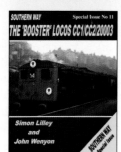
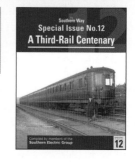
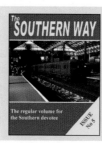
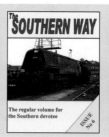
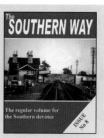